GUARANTEED FULL EMPLOYMENT

A Proposal for Achieving
Continuous Work
Opportunity
for All, Without Inflation,
Through
"Economic Performance
Insurance" (EPI)

Selected & Edited
from the Writings
of
JOHN H.G. PIERSON
by
LEONORA STETTNER

NORTH RIVER PRESS, INC.
Croton-on-Hudson, New York

Library of Congress Cataloging in Publication Data

Pierson, John Herman Groesbeck, 1906-
    Guaranteed full employment.

    Bibliography: p.
    1. United States—Full employment policies. 2. Pierson,
John Herman Groesbeck, 1906-   . I. Stettner,
Leonora, 1914-   . II. Title. III. Title: Economic
performance insurance.
HC106.5.P5386 1985   339.5′0973   85-4827
ISBN 0-88427-059-9

Acknowledgments

Excerpts from the works by John H.G. Pierson listed below are reprinted by permission of the publishers:

Full Employment (New Haven: Yale University Press, 1941)

Full Employment and Free Enterprise (Washington, D.C.: Public Affairs Press, 1947)

Insuring Full Employment. A United States Policy for Domestic Prosperity and World Development (New York: Viking Press, 1964)

Essays on Full Employment, 1942-1972 (Metuchen, N.J.: Scarecrow Press, 1972)

Full Employment Without Inflation. Papers on the Economic Performance Insurance (EPI) Proposal (Allanheld, Osmun, 1980)

Excerpts from the author's "Economic Performance Insurance" which appeared in the February 20, 1983 issue of *Greenwich Time* are reprinted by permission of the publisher, Connecticut Newspapers, Inc.
Excerpts from the author's "Full Employment is Vital" which appeared in the December 8, 1983 issue of *Greenwich News* are reprinted by permission of the publisher.

CONTENTS

"We are in a long pause between the historic discovery that depressions aren't acts of God and the awareness that cycles and unemployment can be abolished altogether."[1]

Editor's Preface

Economists never cease theorizing about, and politicians never cease experimenting with, all sorts of economic nostrums. But the major economic problems confronting the world—as periodically highlighted at international "summits"—are still the same as they have been over many decades: mass unemployment, inflation, budget deficits, high interest rates, crippling labor unrest, destruction of nonrenewable natural resources, fluctuating foreign exchange rates and trade balances accompanied by excessive protectionism, poverty at home and in the Third World, astronomical defense budgets for a deadly arms race.

No doubt most of us can agree that of all these economic ills, involuntary unemployment is the most serious because of its direct and immediate impact on people in terms of destruction of their personalities through poverty, loss of economic security and status, and increased discrimination on grounds of sex, race, or age—to say nothing of the incalculable waste of human resources, loss of output and tax revenues, and increased public expenditures.

But there is another compelling reason for according first priority to the problem of unemployment. This is the argument that has been consistently put forward for a very long time by John Pierson—namely that elimination of unemployment in the United States is also a prerequisite for success in tackling the other difficulties mentioned above. Pierson's thesis is that the achievement of continuous and assured full employment would at the same time make a major contribution toward minimizing poverty, controlling inflation and high interest rates, moderating the struggle between workers and employers, fighting pollution and destruction of the environment, and promoting the kind of international collaboration and mutually beneficial expansion of world trade which is basic to any hope for multilateral disarmament.

Moreover, the United States could take this giant step for-

1

ward at any time, by its own volition; *no need in this case to wait upon international agreements.*

Pierson acknowledges that many brave and constructive efforts have been made over the years to eliminate un-employment, albeit to no avail. Indeed he endorses many of the neo-Keynesian diagnoses and proposed remedies that have characterized those efforts. But what is different and additional about his analysis and his proposal is his stress on the role of *expectations* in the economy, and hence on the possibility, as well as the need, for creating an in-surance mechanism to *guarantee* a full-employment level of economic activity.

It is not good enough, he argues, for governments merely to exert their "best efforts" to minimize unemployment. Because of the many hazards blocking the path of good intentions—ranging from honest differences of view on correct policies to unexpected events like oil-price shocks—something more reliable than pious hopes and unsecured promises is required to engender the kind of expectations that will *sustain* a full-employment level of economic activity. Investors, managers, trade unions and customers cannot be relied on to make expansionary de-cisions unless they are truly confident of the markets, or job opportunities, or incomes which will in the end justify such decisions.

Hence Pierson's proposal that the government, instead of just making its "best efforts," should provide an absolute guarantee of full employment. He has labeled the mech-anism which he would recommend for guaranteeing full employment "Economic Performance Insurance," or EPI for short.

Under EPI, Congress would annually review, and then accept or else modify, the President's recommendation on two commitments. One would be for the level of employ-ment which would provide jobs for all those able and will-ing to work; the other, for the level of consumer spending calculated to create a demand just sufficient to sustain that level of employment. Downward and upward spirals would then no longer occur. The economic expectations and effects generated by these two commitments would tend, reciprocally, toward achieving the targeted levels; but in the event of a shortfall or an excess in either level, the President would automatically set in motion certain compensatory measures—previously agreed to by Congress—to close the gap.

Pierson is convinced that such a full-employment guarantee, which would be politically *neutral,* is also politically feasible. It would be fully compatible with U.S. traditions, including the tradition of democratic determination through the legislative process of the particular mix of public with private activity which on balance is favored by the members of our free-enterprise market economy.

Economic policies would as usual be determined by the American people through their representatives in Congress. Congress would as usual enact all economic legislation—both the *compensatory measures* called for by EPI as such, and the *basic economic policies* as threshed out over the years by Congress. (Those basic policies would be unaffected by the guarantee except for the useful "feedback" effect from the operations of the guarantee system; i.e., the latter would help pinpoint what the current basic difficulties in the economy really were—a skewed income distribution, or overly burdensome government regulations, or anything else—and so would throw into sharper perspective the relative need for various new basic measures.)

The President's role in the process—apart from submitting his recommendations in the first place—would be not to intervene at his own discretion but to have his Administration react automatically if and when necessary in response to the flashing of the predetermined signals. At those points he would be putting into effect, without a further Congressional mandate, compensatory measures previously agreed by Congress.

The pages that follow bring together excerpts from five books and a number of articles on full employment which

John Pierson has published since 1941. The excerpts do not pretend to convey the color and sense of depth to be found in his original writings, but have been selected with a view to distilling the essence of his proposal. It is interesting to note that aside from minor changes of emphasis the essential elements of his thinking have not altered from the time of his first attempt to set down the conditions under which unemployment would not exist. Thus his proposal is "new," not chronologically, but in the sense that it has never been seriously debated. In my opinion, that proposal is more timely than ever before.

The structure of what follows is fourfold. Sections 1, 2 and 3 develop the central concept and purpose of a full-employment guarantee. Sections 4, 5 and 6 describe the Economic Performance Insurance proposal. Sections 7, 8 and 9 deal with the implications of the proposal for inflation, for the mix between the public and private sectors, and for international transactions. Finally Section 10 projects an "action program" for putting the proposal into effect at short notice.

As will appear, that program would (1) amend the Employment Act of 1946 as modified by the Full Employment and Balanced Growth Act of 1978, and would (2) ready the procedures for starting and stopping supplementary public works and services, and for raising and lowering consumer buying power—procedures to be used when necessary for maintaining the designated overall employment and consumer spending levels. Then (3) the already indicated year-by-year legislative and executive action for deciding and maintaining those levels would come into play.

Grateful acknowledgement is made of the generous assistance received from those who helped finance the production and first distribution of this book by contributing to the Q Street Fund.

LEONORA STETTNER

1.
Full Employment is the Central Issue

I have two quite simple propositions that I want to make. The first is that we ought to guarantee full employment in the United States. And the second is that it can be done.[2]

According to the view long urged by John Pierson, the need to establish full employment on a permanent basis is the heart of the economic problem confronting the United States. Full employment, as he sees it, is much more than just one of a number of high-priority goals.

It certainly is that, most of all because of the deep meaning the opportunity to work has for the individual person. But there is also, Pierson keeps saying, its pivotal, *strategic* importance in a wider sense. In guaranteeing full employment the United States would hold the key to progress on many other domestic fronts as well, and beyond that, to dramatic gains in international relations.

> ... one must go deeper than many people who deplore involuntary unemployment normally do. What they see is that full employment is a labor goal, and that the unemployment numbers published periodically are more sensitive politically than most of the other numbers in the kaleidoscopic national statistical picture. What they miss is the connection with the viability of our whole socioeconomic system.[3]

This emphasis of Pierson's on what is at stake distinguishes him from other full-employment advocates almost as much as does the solution he offers. Pierson himself emphasizes that he is not suggesting that other economists are wrong—only that they have been looking in directions that are different. "My hope is, naturally, not just that they *would* find the same answer if they were asking the same question, but that some of them *will* in fact pose that question."[4]

The present section will examine this emphasis and the reasons for it, as given in passages from his writings at various times.

Full employment is essential in the first place, Pierson argues, as a prerequisite for *personal dignity and individual fulfillment.*

> How does one convey the *intrinsic* significance of full employment? One can try by stripping away common misconceptions. Full employment does not mean forcing any man or woman to work, or providing jobs for people not able to work or not honestly seeking to. Nor does it mean having nobody unemployed at all, since obviously in any dynamic society some designated small percentage of "frictional" unemployment is necessary to accommodate labor turnover. But it does mean having no more unemployment than that, so as not to have people up against a blank wall. Surely, if the pursuit of happiness is meant to be for everybody, we must abolish involuntary unemployment and have full employment for its own sake![5]

> You can't pursue happiness very far if you need a job and jobs are not to be had. You could, however, pursue it under permanent full employment.[6]

> Any definition of opportunity that leaves out the opportunity to work is simply not good enough to fulfill the promises implicit in the American dream.[7]

> . . . involuntary unemployment in a free society destroys personality . . . our whole society will tend to grow weak if this process continues. Many hard-core jobless will turn to crime; others will become demoralized to the point where they expect, or perhaps even want, nothing better than to live a life on the dole. . . .

> Income maintenance programs can't prevent this, since the urge to take part in society's active business (not the "work ethic" but something more universal) remains defeated at every turn. From a humane point of view this is as fundamental a criticism of our economic system as could be imagined.[8]

A closely related benefit is the contribution that full employment can make to the *abolition of poverty*. Unemployment and economic instability imply "widening circles of poverty from lack of work income and from the ruin of many fixed-income recipients by inflation."[9]

Abolishing individual and family poverty in the United States would be enormously simplified under continuing full employment because of the great increase in the amount of paid labor—and, incidentally, the lessened chances for certain employers to pay substandard wages. While special income-support programs would still be needed, since many people cannot and should not work, our present antipoverty effort could be drastically curtailed.[10]

. . . the poverty gap could be more than half closed if we had (1) the *assurance* of "useful employment opportunities, including self-employment, for those able, willing, and seeking to work," coupled with a strengthened program to help willing but not-so-able persons to become able; and (2) higher pay at the lower levels, both directly through improved minimum wage legislation and indirectly through the influence that the full employment itself would exert on the labor market. . . .

The disappearance of excess unemployment in the usual sense would of course raise the annual earnings of many more persons than are out of work at any one moment of time.

Also eliminated would be that considerable position of *part-time* employment (with low earnings) which is involuntary too. There are apparently, moreover, at least half a million other persons in the country who would be counted as additional unemployed today were it not that they have become demoralized by the difficulty of getting a job and have stopped "seeking to work." . . .

With continuous opportunity to get a decent job, however, plus a way to train and become qualified for it, most of the now discouraged, ill-equipped people would become employed earners.[11]

[In short] Even in terms of earnings alone—of what the additional opportunities to work would directly and indi-

7

rectly contribute toward the raising of money incomes above the poverty level . . . an assurance of really full employment would be enormously helpful.[12]

Pierson is equally concerned about the injustice and the consequent *social and economic tensions* caused by unemployment which he sees as a serious threat to the fabric of society.

> . . . our business cycles and unemployment are causing divisions that could prove fatal to the nation in the end. Recessions, actualized or even merely anticipated, often impel powerful organizations in business, labor, and agriculture to push their financial claims too vigorously and get into serious conflict with the general interest—usually by causing more price inflation. Editors and highly placed government officials will then ask those organizations to show responsibility. But it is safe (although unpopular) to say that the concept of responsibility will never take very firm root with the parties concerned until the government itself assumes its own responsibility for holding the economy at a satisfactory level.[13]

> Involuntary unemployment . . . virtually compels our major interest groups—labor, farmers, business—to take certain actions and espouse certain policies that run counter to the interests of our economy and society as a whole: premature shortening of the work week, trade restrictions, and low break-even points are some good examples.[14]

> Business investment depends on expectations concerning markets for final products in future years. The wage increases and fringe benefits sought by trade unions reflect not only the current state of the economy but the very fact or existence of the business cycle, since that is what necessitates the construction in good times of all sorts of buffers against bad times to come. Consumers' decisions to spend or to save change markedly with cyclical swings. And these are only the most obvious examples of how the expected future always influences—and often disrupts—the economic present.[15]

Clearly, much more is at issue than "dollar considerations"—notably, the relation between inadequate job opportunity and *discrimination* on the basis of race, sex, age, and other factors.

> Involuntary unemployment . . . makes much more difficult the nation's effort to combat discrimination—prime source of injustice, social tensions, and international suspicion.[16]

> The drive for equal employment opportunity—not to speak of affirmative action on jobs—simply cannot hope for real success without continuing full employment. The efforts must surely be persevered in anyway, but they will truly succeed only when the supply of job opportunity is large enough to match the *total* demand.[17]

> Inadequate employment opportunity has . . . been widening our ominous social divisions. We have all along been suffering, subconsciously at least, from internal strains caused by unduly keen competition for scarce jobs.

> The symptoms are familiar: a little too much pressure on older workers to retire before they wanted or could afford to, a little too little consideration for young entrants into the labor market, and above all the fact that blacks have always been the last to be hired in a boom and the first to be let go in a recession.[18]

Mass unemployment furthermore involves senseless waste that in turn seriously *impairs the infrastructure of the economy.* Pierson emphasizes that unemployment has resulted in "astronomical social waste from nonproduction, as shown for instance in our amazing inability to afford decent public services."[19]

> . . . take our self-evident need for big investments in city rehabilitation, mass transport, conservation, energy research, low-cost housing, education, and health. Think how the wastes of *non*production are limiting what our society can afford to undertake (whether on a private, government-assisted, or government-sponsored basis) in these and other important fields.[20]

> Current services are needed as well as capital investment. For example, many municipal services (street cleaning and sanitation, police protection, mail delivery, parks and rec-

reational facilities, clinics and hospitals, etc.) are very much undermanned.

Moreover these services too use a good deal of relatively unskilled labor, the kind whose outlook is the most precarious today.

Much of this socially essential work should be carried out by the private sector, and much of the rest by state and local government, largely with funds obtained on a revenue-sharing basis from the federal government—a highly desirable new method of financing . . . offered for trial by President Nixon in his antipoverty program. The implied federal partnership and initiative will certainly have to be supplemented, however, by direct federal spending as well.[21]

Even more serious, Pierson points out, is the danger that the fear of unemployment poses for the *natural physical environment.*

The physical environment will remain in grave danger as long as those who pollute or otherwise destroy it are handled with kid gloves for fear of throwing more workers (and managers) out of work. By contrast, that crucial dilemma too would be resolved under the only kind of full employment acceptable in a country with our traditions, namely a policy based on an assured full-employment market.[22]

It is ironical that environmentalists, advocating a course where the stakes are the real quality of our existence and perhaps existence itself, a course which moreover could itself contribute handsomely toward providing the additional jobs that we now need, should be so hampered by fears about the economic consequences of their proposals. But they are.[23]

For the environment, the practical issue today is not whether the long-term investments that are so critically needed to create a more habitable world would provide the vast numbers of new jobs that environmentalists themselves foresee; of course they would! Rather, it is whether enough of them can be carried out. For the likelihood is that many of them will *not* be carried out soon in the absence of an *independently* legislated policy of guaranteed full employment with inflation control. Only a policy like that would assure the existence, elsewhere in the economy, of the jobs needed to offset those that are lost when environmentally dangerous or wasteful industries have to be shut down; and would see to it that certain prices were lowered, elsewhere, to offset the increases in costs and prices that the introduction of antipollution equipment often makes necessary.[24]

Finally, Pierson's experience with international trade negotiations and with Third World problems convinced him that *the international stakes* are already almost as high as the domestic stakes and may ultimately be higher.

But he has always maintained that full employment in the United States has to be secured by *domestic* means, and so the main point his proposal makes *internationally* is that U.S. full employment, because of the general significance of the U.S. economy, is indirectly essential for the rest of the world too. His argument is not that the rest of the world should also adopt the proposal—in fact he has always stressed that he was not venturing to say what other countries should do, but only what the United States should.

> Since American industrialists and farmers so often lack an adequate market, our nation cannot be a reliable good neighbor. In our intention, we are liberal traders and generous givers besides; but in practice we are as apt as not to restrict imports that Third World and other countries need as foreign-exchange-earning exports, and to force our exports on them, and to claim poverty at home as excuse for limiting our aid to the less developed countries and our cooperation with them.
>
> Dumping one's unsolved difficulties somewhere else is not risk-free. We may not escape the consequences in the long run. Today, even the balance between peace and war is affected by our purely domestic troubles. For example, if security reasons for selling arms abroad happen to be doubtful or worse, we often sell those arms anyway to bolster American jobs and cut the trade deficit.
>
> All of the above actions combined have left us by now with

few real friends around the world. Friends that, if we had them all about us—as we might again—could bring great pressure to bear on the Russians to match us in a far-reaching mutual arms reduction program once we proposed one.[25]

Assured full employment does appear to be possible—here, in the country where it matters most. We need not risk national bankruptcy or inflation in order to get it. We need not overturn our individualistic habits and institutions. We can solve this particular problem any time we like, without international negotiations. We would derive from assured full employment new freedom and power to deal with our other problems in a confident, firm, and generous manner.[26]

2.

Full Employment Has To Be Guaranteed

The second of Pierson's most fundamental arguments is that continuous full employment will not—cannot—be achieved in the absence of a firm government commitment, together with administrative procedures for implementing that commitment.

Failure to acknowledge the need for this "insurance" approach mostly stems, he believes, from an unwillingness to concede that full employment *is* the central issue.

> The economic concept makers are gone. Loyal bands of their followers battle over questions such as whether monetary or fiscal policy is more important, whether the structural approach is the one that really makes sense, whether everybody is a Keynesian now or Keynesianism is dead. Congress and the Administration find the range of conceptual options uncomfortably narrow as a basis for action.
>
> The nub of the problem is that none of the concept makers has squarely faced the question that, in our time, needs to be put first. That question is: *how can we have permanent full employment in the United States, and have it without inflation, by means that won't weaken but instead will strengthen the private enterprise market system?*
>
> Full employment *is* the key to the answer. Some of my fellow economists avoid this conclusion by taking refuge behind the idea that unemployment and price inflation are locked into a *trade-off* (the Phillips curve), so that one has to go up if the other comes down. Some others who do envisage economic stabilization at full employment seem to think that it can only be approached indirectly—by tackling a series of other, mostly egalitarian, social goals directly and then (if successful there!) extracting *full employment as a sort of by-product*. It is as though they were a little ashamed to advocate full employment head-on, of treating it as worthy of their determined effort in its own right.[27]

The Trade-Off Excuse

The "trade-off" is not an immutable law of our economic life. America has not run out of easy ways of doing things. . . . The underlying concept of the trade-off came into vogue as the concern over our inflation spread. There is nothing complex about it in principle. Business and labor both like to charge what the traffic will bear, and so the high demand, piled higher for several years by huge military spending, bid up wages and prices. Eventually, in fairness to fixed-income receivers if for no other reason, there had to be a decision to apply the brakes and check the demand—direct fiscal brakes of less spending and more taxing, indirect monetary ones of fewer bank loans at higher rates of interest. But this sort of braking action, while at first sight it might seem to be having practically no effect whatever, is bound in due course to slow production too in some degree and cause some workers to be laid off. Hence the conclusion is drawn that some sort of trade-off between major *desiderata* is inevitable; if we want more price stability, we must also—so it is said—accept more unemployment.[28]

The trade-off is a concept deriving from the days of our great depressions. When one of those "acts of God" occurred . . . workers by the millions were thrown on the street and businessmen found their markets absolutely flat. Wages and prices certainly came down. Today, while shunning a return to such conditions, the economic doctors are still preoccupied with the thought that a milder dose of the same old medicine will be just enough to hold prices reasonably steady. Pressure on people but not to much pressure. Just a *slight* twist of the arm. The bullfight without really killing the bull.

But the foundations of that hope are extremely shaky, to say the least. Statistics?—the evidence cannot help but be inconclusive. . . . Logic?—here the case for the trade-off is especially weak. Why expect our powerful unions to knuckle under in their wage demands if unemployment rises moderately? A response of that kind seems no more probable in the world of today than persistence of upward wage pressure coupled now with rising pressure for more unemployment relief and larger welfare payments. *Ultimately*, to be sure, and *at certain levels* of unemployment and shrunken demand, a real economic squeeze would be bound to produce its intended results, ending the inflation. But what does that mean; hard times of what duration and to what extent—and expectable under what political auspices? Consider also this haunting question; how can anyone say with confidence how much unemployment would still have to be retained as a permanent warning after the shake-down was over?. . .

To disparage the trade-off approach to policy would be a great pity if there were no better alternative. Fortunately, however, there is one. That better alternative, I submit, is to grasp the nettle firmly by guaranteeing full employment at all times, meanwhile negotiating a suitable understanding with labor, business, and farm leaders. By "suitable understanding" I mean one in which it was agreed that the *quid* for the *quo* of guaranteed full employment and continuously adequate total demand for goods and services was the acceptance by those leaders of some kind of reasonable guideposts, guidelines, or frame of reference for the processes traditionally followed in establishing their selling prices.[29]

The By-product Fallacy

We are in a long pause between the historic discovery that depressions aren't acts of God and the awareness that cycles and unemployment can be abolished altogether. In my opinion this pause is needlessly prolonged by three factors: (1) As just said, the worst dangers from unemployment have been largely ignored. (2) So long as the *modus operandi* has not yet been understood, some persons suppose that guaranteed full employment would be too rigid or too disruptive—that it would stifle free enterprise, give the Administration too difficult a task, rob Congressional committees of their prerogatives, and so on. In fact, no such results need follow, as I will show. (3) Finally, many economists have seriously underestimated the difference between combating unemployment and really ending it.

All sorts of policies, taken in isolation, would stimulate the economy and combat unemployment, and not a few have been overplayed as answers—not necessarily by exaggeration of their positive effects but by disregard of all the elements of uncertainty as to events and other legislation

15

and even their own more indirect repercussions. For example, liberals (with whom I usually agree, on most issues) often talk as though full employment could be had as a side-effect of the extra mass purchasing power or government spending to be gained by winning the *other* victories they hope to achieve.

Here we have the by-product theory of full employment. As Sir William Beveridge put it, "If we attack with determination, unity and clear aim the four giant evils of Want, Disease, Ignorance and Squalor, we shall destroy in the process their confederate—the fifth giant of Idleness enforced by mass employment." But Sir William saw clearly that he had to invoke "unity" to envisage an end even to "mass" unemployment, and no unity in support of the liberal—or any other!—program is in sight in America today.[30]

The Inadequacy of a Mere Full-Employment "Goal"

There have been a great many proposals for *trying* to achieve or maintain full employment, or for having a level of employment "as high as possible." The audible support for that objective must by now be as almost as great as the audible condemnation of sin. . . .

The trouble with a full-employment program of that description is that it all too easily becomes a maximum-employment program. Not in the strong sense in which, to quote from the Employment Act, "there will be afforded useful employment opportunities, including self-employment, for those able, willing and seeking to work," but in the weak sense in which "maximum" is tantamount to saying that the government will do, as a practical matter, the best that it can.[31]

Actually, current theories and proposals simply will not *unaided* give us guaranteed full employment. The better ones would, if enacted, help to reduce unemployment, but they uniformly fail to provide a final "insurance" device, something to make *sure*. For guaranteed full employment *two* things are needed: not only policies to give us a reasonably good first approximation, but also a clearly formulated last-resort "insurance" plan in the form of *contingent or standby devices that are certain to be called into action to the extent that the first approximation fails to satisfy the guarantee.*

Even if some Prsidential economic adviser should calculate "perfectly," Congress would find reasons to change the program, which consequently, barring coincidence, would end up either smaller or larger than it started out to be. Nor would Congress often correct perfectly an *im*perfect Presidential program. All approaches that depend on having exactly the right full-employment program formulated ahead of time are, therefore, inherently fallible. This much could no doubt be shown mathematically.

Of course our government really proceeds on a different premise altogether, the premise that economic fluctuations, when not held sufficiently in check by the built-in stabilizers like unemployment compensation, can be corrected by introducing contra-cyclical measures on an *ad hoc* basis. Thus, when the President or Congress thinks that a recession threatens, a bill will be introduced to lower certain taxes or perhaps pay out tax refunds. But this approach must fail too, if only because of the excruciatingly long time that tax changes always take to become law, given the conflicts of opinion.[32]

Social goals are bound to be controversial. Therefore, attainment of the uncontroversially right economic goal, stability at full employment, has to be assured independently—in particular, it must not be left to stand or fall by the outcome of the perennial struggle over the mix of public and private spending.[33]

It is an illusion to suppose that things will go right if only "we" can get "them" out of office and substitute "our" program. True, some economic ideas are far better than some others; a politician who merely tells you that his is better can sometimes be right. Judged, however, by the much stiffer test that what is needed is to solve the pivotal problem, all the partisan measures in sight and all the *ad hoc* proposals in general are absolutely deficient. As they must be.

This is not meant as disparagement of the other virtues they may have. It is simply to state the truism that we cannot be sure to have full employment unless we are willing to make sure.

We have multiple objectives and—in our world of side effects, conflicts, and chance—the solution of the pivotal problem gets lost for lack of a specific device to make sure that it doesn't get lost. Any claim that full employment can be won and kept as the by-product of something else (an expanded welfare package, for instance, or taking the shackles off business) is false or simply naïve.[34]

The Insurance Approach

In my opinion, we have outlived the time when we can afford uncertainty in this particular area. It is an area in which we need to be able to count on having continuous success from now on. For that, I believe that nothing less than "national income insurance," in the general sense of some form of economy-wide guarantee, will do.[35]

. . . to give a binding *promise* is something quite other than to set a *goal* and then (in the face of wrong forecasts, unexpected events, and divided counsels) merely do "the best that we can" toward achieving it![36]

Not even the most sophisticated econometric model pretends to incorporate all the significant knowable variables . . . And then there remain the unknowables—bad weather, wars, concerted foreign action on our oil supplies, etc.—fully capable of upsetting the best calculations. . . .

Look at the matter this way: Good economic advisers are not enough without a definite, recurring legislative procedure. Such a procedure is not enough without well-selected targets. Those targets are not enough unless they are firm. Firmness is impossible without contingent arrangements.[37]

We may need permanent full employment, but can we have it?

The answer starts with the fact that we certainly cannot get it from any known liberal Democratic formula or from a conservative Republican one—from Keynes or monetarism or supply-side economics or any other special and hence limited approach. Instead, we have to get it by adopting a new, essentially general "insurance" approach—*not special and limited, not a speculative remedy at all*—and by keeping that policy in effect all the time, above politics, let the liberal-conservative tide on other issues swing as it may.[38]

Here is an intricate knot that cannot be untied but has to be cut. Yet it can be cut by adopting an "insurance" approach that takes the final results of all the moves and cross-currents into account. Economic Performance Insurance, I have called this proposal, or EPI.[39]

The Impact of Technological Advance

With the onward march of technology, production shortages should continue to recede and the civilian output to rise, the drain from wars and military buildup permitting. So much so that it will be necessary to spread the work by progressively shorter work weeks, longer paid vacations, extended education and training, sabbatical periods, and so on.

Seeing this, some people have tended to push the panic button, envisaging the early displacement of man by machines in all production. According to them, automation has already made the system of income distribution based on contributions to production, and especially on work performed, wholly untenable. "We don't need people as producers," someone said (one wonders about the "we"), "we just need them as consumers."

Drawn in this manner, the picture is undoubtedly overdrawn. The need for continued hard work, not only to create a decent America but also to help raise up the pitifully low living standards in the underdeveloped parts of the world, is much greater than this view would have us suppose. Let us not, therefore, announce the demise of the present income distribution system too far in advance.

Nevertheless the time is coming when the realities of production will enforce frank recognition of the need for at least a hybrid system of distribution. And leadership in our present time of momentous changes should recognize that fact. Political leaders have to deal with what people really believe and want.

The newer "life style," less addicted to work, is the case in point here. Since this new outlook rests on the underlying changes in technology—whose dependence on past *work* is, of course, irrelevant—it is solidly based and will not go away. Hence it cannot well be ignored.[40]

The Guarantee Approach as an Umbrella Policy

[An] issue arises whenever someone thinks that my proposal is against, or perhaps disregards the importance of,
his or her proposal. That is a misconception in principle.
EPI is an umbrella policy, potentially consistent with any
and all other measures, be they "liberal" or "conservative,"
for promoting prosperity and stability at the full-employment level.[41]

The EPI idea is not in conflict with others that aim to make
our economic system perform closer to capacity, with fewer
fluctuations, and with less inflation. EPI would simply be
an umbrella policy, for use in conjunction with all other
policies currently in effect, to make sure that the wanted
economic stabilization results were in fact obtained. It
would do so by assigning responsibility for quantitative
definition of the results needed and by arranging matters
so that, when events had shown how our economy was
actually performing at a given moment, the gap would be
filled or the excess trimmed away, if either existed. Thus
EPI is not a "special" solution for full employment; it is the
"general case" solution.[42]

. . . an effective set of compensatory devices is, indeed, the
very thing that would focus attention most sharply on the
need to improve our basic, long-term policies with a view
to having them better encourage business initiative, raise
purchasing power among those who now have too little,
and reverse the inroads that monopolistic practices have
been making into potentially competitive areas. All those
who are unsatisfied with second-best solutions—in this case
heavier use of compensatory devices and larger budget
deficits than would really be necessary for full employment
if those long-term policies were stronger—would have the
rationale of their further proposals greatly clarified. Moreover, the actual merits of their proposed measures could
be more easily tested, once the optical illusions born of the
business cycle itself had disappeared.[43]

. . . the optimum-allocation problem does not have to be
solved as a prerequisite for solving the full-employment
problem. . . . society might as well regard allocation as a
perennial problem. Not so with full employment, the conditions for which can be established once and for all.[44]

To make the point more informally, there's no good reason why our country should not secure full employment, which almost everyone needs and wants, even while it keeps many of its more controversial options open.[45]

3.

Economic Performance Insurance

Economic Performance Insurance is basically and deceptively simple in concept and in proposed operation—"deceptively" because its very simplicity has over the years led some sophisticated readers to look for hidden snags. Pierson himself began by calling it "an idea not so easy to grasp—that the United States could . . . abolish unemployment without giving up its decentralized economic initiative."[46]

In this section his proposal will be described in broad outline. In the following three sections its basic features will be presented in greater detail.

The Objective

> The policy we need would be aimed first at securing guaranteed full employment in the United States; that is, at assuring that everyone who is able and seeking to work will always have that opportunity. This, however, is not something that should or can happen in isolation. The policy must put an end to deflation generally and to the business cycle, must minimize price inflation, and must really favor individual initiative and private enterprise, not just pay them lip service.[47]

> Our federal government needs to end the present guesswork, confusion, and delay by substituting responsible advance policy decisions (1) on certain precisely formulated goals and (2) on standby measures to assure achievement of those goals.[48]

> The common theme of all these papers is: (1) that our national interests require the development of a line of policy whereby we can *assure* the continued maintenance of full employment without inflation; and (2) that such a line of policy, to conform with the American spirit, must be based on an overall insurance approach emphasizing personal freedom, sustained high consumption, full attention

to public works and services required for the common welfare, and a minimum of other government operations and interventions.[49]

The General Concept

What I am proposing is the imposition of control over the level of operation of the economy as a whole, not over the individual producer except as necessary to avoid price or wage extortion in special cases. The new element here is the concept of "economic performance insurance." This would involve guaranteeing bottom and top limits to employment and consumer spending. Once the President and Congress had aligned those two targets for the year ahead, final adjustments of the actual aggregates would be brought about without further Congressional debate if and as current statistics showed them to be required.[50]

It may be remembered that the Classical School of economists held that full employment tended to occur automatically, with supply and demand reciprocally sustaining each other. In this belief they were wrong (since they ignored the savings-investment problem and the problem of imperfect competition). They were not so far wrong, however, but that it is possible to create by means of a system of prearranged, minor, contingent adjustments at *both* ends of the production-consumption process a practical modern analogue to the unreal abstraction they had in mind.[51]

. . . a full-employment market economy will resemble the world of present-day American experience, not the hypothetical world of Ricardo and the classical economists, so far as concerns the nature of the individual producer's markets, but will resemble the Ricardian and not the actual world in possessing a stable total market at a level ruling out any involuntary idleness.[52]

Everyone knows that a life-sustaining "circular flow" of production and demand at the full-employment level is impossible, in view of monopolistic interferences with the market mechanism and the absence of any special reason why intended savings and actual investments should add to the same total. But what counts today is that we could reinstate that Classical idea in a practical way by constantly attending to the two aggregates, employment and con-

sumer spending. Each of them would then strongly reinforce the other, leaving the final adjustments to be rather
small, as long as the rest of our economic and social policies
were in reasonable balance.[53]

To understand "economic performance insurance" or EPI,
think of our economic system as driven by two engines:
production, which provides the jobs and generates income,
and spending (consumption and investment spending),
which motivates production and employment by providing
a current and prospective market for goods and services.
Each engine pumps out to the other and each depends for
fuel on what the other pumps out. All this is familiar, of
course. So is the fact that the system doesn't tend to keep
running at a full-employment rate automatically, as the
Classical School assumed.

What is not so familiar is the idea that a balanced circular
flow at the full-employment rate, while it won't come about
naturally, can nevertheless be created artificially by tuning
both engines occasionally so that each reinforces the other
with optimum support. Once they are revved up by stages
to the right pitch, neither one can easily get very far out
of line, and comparatively minor tuning should then suf-
fice. Furthermore, the system's chronic obstructions and
leaks will then be considerably easier to identify and correct; hence a prospect of still less tuning. This in essence
is the EPI idea.

EPI would *not* rely on trying to find remedies after something important has gone wrong, or do the opposite and
set about filling "prospective gaps" glimpsed in forecasts,
or pay attention to just one engine and let the other take
care of itself. Instead, EPI would have our government,
year by year, prescribe an operating rate for each engine
separately. It would equip our system with two throttles,
one on each engine. And it would issue standing orders for
each throttle to be opened or closed a little whenever that
engine would otherwise fail to hold to its prescribed operating rate.[54]

Implementation of the Proposal

What EPI would do is amend present general policy legislation governing the annual procedure aimed at full em-

ployment, so that thereafter: (1) the President would each year recommend specific levels of employment and consumer spending to be guaranteed, and methods to be used as necessary for honoring those guarantees; (2) Congress would then accept or modify those Presidential recommendations; and (3) the Executive Branch, without further Congressional intervention, would execute the given mandate by activating the approved standby measures to the extent found necessary.[55]

Just two target levels would be set every year to be actually guaranteed and firmly adhered to—not razor-edged levels but suitably narrow ranges or bands between an anti-inflationary ceiling above and an anti-recessionary floor below. The two things so targeted would be total employment and total consumer spending.

Employment would be set at the level judged by the President and Congress as corresponding to full employment. Consumer spending would be set at the level that, when added to the best-guess prospective amounts for private domestic investment, government purchases, and (plus or minus) net exports, ought to clear the production markets at a full-employment rate of production or GNP, allowing for whatever price level increase appeared unavoidable.

The full employment would strongly tend toward yielding the income needed for the targeted consumer spending, while the chosen amount of consumer spending (coupled with the business, government, and foreign spending) would strongly tend to regenerate the full employment. But those are probabilities and approximations only, and so they would have to be backed up.

Thus, whenever employment missed its target on the downside, additional public "shelf" projects would be started, and whenever it missed on the upside, some projects would be returned to the shelf. Similarly, whenever consumer spending fell too low or rose too high, contingent fiscal measures—such as modified income tax withholding or a special consumer sales bonus/sales tax—would be put into effect to increase or reduce consumers' disposable income. The statistical series available in Washington are quite adequate for both these tasks.

The crux is that in either case the action would be "automatic," that is, it would be instituted by the Executive branch without further debate in Congress, which would have had the last word each year in setting the mandatory targets and standby balancing devices.[56]

The EPI regulators should clearly not be submitted to constant strain. In the analogy, engineers should be out on the lines finding ways to improve the flow in both directions and so reduce the need for throttle adjustments at either end. Visualize here the enactment, over time, of tax reforms and other measures that spread purchasing power and boost consumer spending, plus steadfast help to competition and vigilance against monopolistic restrictions, to keep increased spending from lifting prices instead of production and employment.[57]

Forecasts

One of the harrowing things about many of the economic-policy proposals since the Employment Act was first taken up for consideration has been the degree to which they have depended—or seemed to depend—on forecasting. As the *New York Herald Tribune* said not unkindly in a recent editorial, "With the best will in the world and the greatest storehouse of statistics, Walter Heller can guess wrong. Arthur Goldberg can guess wrong. John Kenneth Galbraith can guess wrong."

Certainly this is true, as they would be the first to concede and as would be equally true of any Republicans serving in the same or other official posts. An insurance approach, however, does not rely unduly on forecasting. The present proposal looks to the use of advance estimates and judgment to arrive at suitable employment and consumer-spending levels to be guaranteed, but governmental compensatory action would be held back to await the unfolding of events. The proposal would lead not to sensing a prospective gap and filling it with a government program, but to prearranging the kind of gap-filling action to be taken only if and when a designated official index moved out of the range which Congress had decided was economically safe. (No one would be under the illusion that that designated index was perfect, either. It would simply be the most suitable index available, and as such would be treated as recording the facts relevant for operations.)[58]

Action would not be triggered by forecasts, since all adjustments of taxes and/or of the "last resort" jobs program would be made only when the accredited national consumer spending and/or employment series of statistics showed that the economy was in fact failing to meet the Congressionally set standards. The adjustments would, however, be made promptly in the prearranged manner then—rather that at the end of long-drawn-out, uncertain, and partly self-defeating political struggles such as have preceded our compensatory tax changes until now.[59]

Summary

For those who are unfamiliar with this concept and proposal, let me quote the shortest summary I have been able to devise so far: ". . . under that approach the Federal Government would state in advance each year (a) the minimum and maximum levels of employment, and (b)—so as to assure private business of a continuously adequate total market—the minimum and maximum levels of private consumer spending, that would without fail be maintained. The government would then use accelerations and decelerations of public services and works as necessary for honoring its commitment under (a), and changes in consumer taxes and/or transfer payments on some predetermined basis as necessary for honoring its commitment under (b)."[60]

4.

The Employment Target and Stabilizer

Here are some passages in which Pierson amplifies his view about what, in a practical sense, "full" employment is, and in which he outlines the procedures for stabilizing actual employment at the target level.

The Minimum Level

> ... where unemployment is involuntary—where a person seeks employment because of the need for the money or because of the need for the sense of participation—that person cannot be left out of account.

> The opportunity indicated by full employment is the opportunity for *all*—all who are prepared to exert themselves in the labor market. Women who want to work and are able to work come within the scope of the concept just as much as men; whether they have husbands working is not the point. . . . Old age is no reason for exclusion from work either, if the desire and the capacity are there. Nor is youth a reason, except to the extent that the employment of young people is, for their protection, subject to legal limitations.[61]

> Apart from labor-force growth due to the changing size and age-composition of the population, an effective full-employment policy would no doubt also bring into the picture at the beginning many persons previously not even on record as wanting to work. No need, however, to attempt the impossible. In the transition period from our present excessive unemployment, the President could if he thought best propose moving up to full employment by stages and reaching it in, for example, the second quarter of the second year.[62]

Frictional Unemployment

The existence of *frictional* unemployment is not, as is sometimes assumed, a negation of full employment—not if the amount is *reasonable* in relation to the existing rates of industrial progress, voluntary job change, entrance of new workers into the labor market, etc. In our dynamic society, that kind of "slack" *does not indicate a job shortage, since nobody is being deprived of the chance to work.* The real question, therefore, as Pierson emphasizes, is whether reasonable figures are being used in estimating the necessary amount of this frictional or transitional unemployment, i.e., what the existing turnover and the existing frictions actually call for.

> . . . the continuous maintenance of full employment [means] no unemployment in excess of the amount decided on in advance by reasonable men as constituting "necessary frictional unemployment."[63]

> [The proposal by the President to Congress for a] minimum level of employment (in terms, presumably, of the seasonally adjusted monthly national total reported by the Department of Labor) would reflect the President's view of the correct statistical definition of full employment for the year ahead. This quantity would be derived by estimating the civilian labor force and subtracting the amount of unemployment that seemed to the President reasonable in the light of production shifts, manpower policies, and labor mobility at the time (the allowance for 'necessary frictional unemployment').[64]

> Structural rigidities in our economy constitute a . . . major reason why those who are close to the problem recognize that the supply side must not be neglected. Demand may be maintained; the need for price and wage moderation may be sufficiently accepted; yet, even so, workers cannot be expected to get together with unlisted work opportunities that in any case call for different skills and are located somewhere else. A smoothly running economy requires a maximum of information about markets, the labor market certainly included, and a maximum of functional and geographical mobility. A full-employment program can indeed still be carried out while serious structural rigities persist—let me emphasize this—but a larger volume of frictional unemployment will have to be allowed for in the definition of full employment than after the rigidities have been sof-

tened or overcome. Moreover, because of various bottle-
necks for skilled manpower, it will be a little harder than
necessary to hold the line on prices.[65]

Matching Supply with Demand for Skills

The underlying concept of course is that there should be
no *involuntary* unemployment, over and above the "necessary frictional" amount. (*Some* small percentage—for people just entering the labor market, or laid off temporarily,
or moving from one job to another—is inevitable under
present methods of counting.) In other words, the objective
is to have a situation in which there will always be job opportunities, at fair levels of pay and under decent working
conditions, for all men and women who are able to work
and who give suitable positive evidence that they want to.
For persons who wish to work but are not able to work
effectively, the better solution appears to be not to "bend"
the concept but rather to provide training and other relevant forms of assistance on a generous scale, to help them
become able.[66]

The proposal . . . envisages . . . that training programs
would stand ready to help anyone to *become* able who
wanted to be but at the moment was not.[67]

. . . there is or should be a national purpose not only to
provide employment opportunities for all those able, willing, and seeking to work but also to fight against so-called
unemployability; that is, to help anyone, "willing" and
"seeking" but not as yet "able," to overcome his or her
inability.[68]

. . . the demand is now more and more for workers with
a high-school or college education supplemented by technical or professional skills, and automation is accelerating
the growth of that emphasis. The unskilled or semiskilled
worker consequently runs into difficulty not only because
the total number of job opportunities is too small but also
because he is not equipped to seize the opportunities that
do exist. In addition, geographical shifts in the location of
industry are occurring—some from what might be loosely
called natural causes, others because the composition of
government defense contracts is changing. Import competition may be expected to cause similar though lesser
changes in the geographical pattern of industry. If the goal

of a disarmament agreement can be achieved, the dislocations are likely to be emphasized considerably more.[69]

As far as training is concerned, however, it is plainly not just the vocational side that is important for meeting the structural adjustment problem. The whole of our educational system is involved, even more completely than is sometimes appreciated. Unskilled workers who have not had a general education, including our young people who drop out of school too early, often have natural aptitudes but still lack the foundation which a superstructure of specialized knowledge usually requires. Anything that will strengthen our general education system in its curriculum or teaching, or remove the existing racial discriminations in education, or expand enrollments at intermediate and higher levels (presupposing that standards are not lowered in the process) will also help to ease the structural difficulties in our labor market.[70]

The Maximum Level

A maximum limit on employment is needed too, as a safeguard against inflation.[71]

Not only should unemployment not rise above the intended rate but it should not fall far below that rate either, lest a too tight, "overemployment" situation be thereby created. Total *employment* should therefore be kept from falling below a certain specified level and also from rising very much above that level. In other words, the commitment would be to hold employment within a defined range or band, above a certain minimum or floor but below a certain maximum or ceiling (and not, of course, at a precise point, which would clearly be impractical). How wide this band should be is a question that needs to be studied. Provisionally—but only as a starting point for discussion—I suggest that a 1 percent variation might create a situation that was neither too loose nor too tight; if at some point the floor were 100 million persons, the ceiling would then be 101 million.[72]

The Target Has to be Politically—Not Theoretically—Correct

When the composition of the labor force is changing rapidly, and the key statistical series are admittedly imperfect,

31

and economic theory fails to supply an applicable definition, who is to say exactly what (small) reported percentage of residual unemployment is the *correct* measure of "full" employment? For practical purposes, however, this entire difficulty vanishes under the EPI method whereby the President and Congress, with all of the doubts and conflicting opinions in plain view, would name the *official* measure, hold performance to *that* throughout the year, and adjust the target numbers in the light of experience one year later.[73]

The fact that no theoretically satisfying definition of "full" employment can be formulated for today's imperfectly competitive labor market is immaterial. Once we agree to maintain full employment without fail, the rigor of the definition becomes operational, not abstract. First, the lobbying by interest groups as Presidential recommendations and Congressional decisions are going forward will (given such agreement) lead to the designation of some particular rate of unemployment or level of employment as being the officially certified equivalent of full employment for the year ahead. Then *that* official standard, whatever it happens to be, must be scrupulously adhered to. This will bear repeating. The rigor of the definition cannot lie in choosing some theoretically satisfying standard (there isn't any), but rather it must lie in absolutely upholding whatever numerical standard has in fact been chosen.

If critics—from labor or business, for instance—then feel that the chosen standard is too loose or too tight to reflect the underlying concept, they can agitate for adjustment of the numbers when the new standard is being set the following year. Thus nobody under these procedures is expected to do the impossible, but the government *is* periodically required to seek a good working answer to the question, declare what it is, commit itself to that answer, and honor that commitment.[74]

The Employment Stabilizer

. . . it is self-evident that a commitment to hold aggregate employment within a pre-announced range would require the Federal Government to stand ready to act as the employer of last resort, i.e. to hire more workers on its own payrolls or under its own contracts and/or to finance State or local govenments (or possibly non-profit organizations) prepared to do that extra hiring. The commitments and action . . . would thus be within the general frame of the concept of a reserve shelf of public works and services. From this "shelf" additional jobs would be drawn when necessary by accelerating work or starting up new projects, and to it some jobs would be "restored" when necessary by declerating existing work or suspending or terminating certain projects.[75]

The reserve shelf should contain service as well as construction projects, since otherwise it often will not be possible to utilize the skills of those who may be temporarily without jobs in private industry, or to derive the maximum public benefit from the compensatory program. All projects included should be clearly useful to the community. Some examples are: work on streets, roads, airports, and terminal facilities; land reclamation, drainage, erosion control, irrigation; construction of libraries and museums; improvement of public forests and parks, including development of fish and game resources; construction of theatres, stadiums, auditoriums; music, theatre, art, and recreation programs; river and harbor work; rural electrification; modernization of public buildings; health and safety inspection and promotion; laboratory research; compilation of municipal and other governmental records and statistics; preparation of maps, catalogues, guides, histories, yearbooks, and directories. Exactly what might be included on the reserve shelf would depend, of course, on what items were scheduled as non-deferable and placed on the regular budget.[76]

Employment on such projects should be on a par with other local employment so far as concerns wage rates for similar types of work and working conditions. It should also be on a par with other employment in the matter of the number of hours worked per week and per month. An incentive to return to private employment as soon as possible would remain, for many persons, because of the manifest impossibility of using individual skills and meeting individual job preferences on public works even as well as this is ordinarily accomplished elsewhere, and, more generally, because of the uncertainty of job tenure on the fill-in program.

This particular uncertainty should be deliberately fostered, through establishment of the principle of priority for private construction and private work in general. When private employers were ready again to expand employment at locally prevailing rates of pay, *et cetera,* they should be assisted to do so by being assigned prior claims to locally available labor (and equipment and materials), as well as to labor available on a voluntary basis through interregional clearance. In other words, the Employment Service should be kept informed by private employers of their prospective needs for labor, and at the proper time this agency should give notice to the Federal Works Agency to reduce or terminate its fill-in operations as rapidly as possible consistent with peserving the value of the work already done.[77]

The reserve shelf should certainly include only works and services of intrinsic value, including activities already being carried out on some level as well as new projects. To enable work to be started and tapered off quickly, undue dependence on equipment with inflexible delivery or operating schedules should be avoided. A wide spectrum of "industry" fields and occupational skills should be represented. The shelf should include local, state, and federal projects, many to be operated on a contract basis by profit-making construction firms or nonprofit agencies. Since it must obviously have nationwide coverage, the geographical apportionment formula for expansions and contractions would raise important questions for the President and Congress to decide. One of the main factors in setting up special work programs today, however, namely differences in the severity of unemployment from area to area, would become far less important for the *reserve* shelf (as distinct from the ongoing "first resort" work against "structural" unemployment in blighted areas etc.) once national full employment was guaranteed.

Although building and maintaining this reserve shelf would be the most laborious undertaking necessitated by EPI, the psychological resistance that similar undertakings have met in the past should largely disappear. Any fear of a creeping governmental encroachment at the expense of private enterprise would be clearly unwarranted under the EPI system, since marginal contractions of publicly sponsored jobs would be as likely to be called for as marginal expansions (i.e., if the consumer spending calculations [explained below] aimed at the midpoint in the guaranteed employment range). And it would be absurd to suggest that adjustments utilizing the reserve shelf could not be very greatly speeded up, once given the will in Washington to keep that device always ready for immediate use.[78]

5.

The Consumer Spending Target

Not a few full-employment advocates have wanted the government to seve as employer of last resort and have let the matter rest there. Pierson has always called that proposal impractical because it is incomplete, and he has added to it his distinctive proposal of a second guarantee—a guarantee of consumer spending. Why? Because the mainspring of private enterprise is and always has been an expected demand for products.

Why Not an Employment Guarantee Alone?

This idea of filling employment gaps from a reserve shelf of public works and services has been around a long time. It is a very good idea. Why isn't it used more? Why aren't the reserve shelves of projects even there? Why does a promise to really use this device as needed only serve to widen the credibility gap?

The reason is not unlike the reason a bird cannot fly on one wing. The employer of last resort is an excellent wing, but the other wing is missing. Private enterprise needs also to be assured that the final market for its products will always be adequately large to enable a full-employment volume of goods and services to be sold.

This is not double-talk or misunderstanding. The economic case against one-wing flying is fundamental. Certainly employment creates income to spend; however, even assuming we had full employment to begin with, no one could say how long the final demand would keep up adequately. Sluggishness—oversaving, if you like—could always appear in the economy, causing demand to turn down, and then employment too unless last-resort jobs were multiplied progressively.[79]

Could not the maintenance of consumer spending be assured by the very act of assuring the maintenance of employment itself, so that a separate underwriting of consumer spending would be superfluous? My answer to this is as follows: The guaranteeing of full employment alone would indeed (assuming it were politically possible) give the prospect that *income* would remain at levels associated with, and in a meaningful sense derived from, full employment. But personal *consumption expenditures* would not be assured of remaining at levels favorable to the *continuation* of full employment. The larger the aggregate of business, governmental, and personal savings, the smaller, of course, the total of personal consumption expenditures. The great danger of over-saving, as I see it, would be precisely the danger that personal consumption expenditures would be too small, even when income was initially at the full-employment level, to keep such a full-employment guarantee from breaking down by reason of the impossibility, under normal peacetime conditions, of boosting government offsets to saving *in form of government expenditures for goods and services* sufficiently to maintain that guarantee. If, however, consumer spending were underwritten and sustained *independently*, at levels high enough to substantially prevent or offset over-saving when it would otherwise occur, the strain leading to breakdown should be absent.[80]

In short, adequate employment cannot be trusted *entirely* to sustain necessary demand, any more than adequate demand can be trusted entirely to sustain employment. The reciprocal feedbacks are there but they are only approximately reliable. So, both key elements must be kept at their right levels independently. Our economy needs two independently strong wings.[81]

If it is not feasible for government to maintain full employment by expanding *its own* demand in the market whenever private demand tends to fall short, the government can instead so regulate its revenues and expenditures that, by and large, *private* demand is prevented from falling short. In the main, this involves expansion when necessary—and also contraction when and if necessary—of *consumer* demand, brought about through government action affecting *directly* the level of purchasing power. Thus the government does not go into competition with business but instead supports the general market for the normal products of business.[82]

The question of feasibility depends . . . on whether or not

aggregate consumer spending is underwritten in addition
to aggregate employment as such. Without that feature, a
policy of guaranteed full employment could involve the
government in so large a degree of direct responsibility for
the creation of jobs—such as expansion of public works,
and perhaps wholesale subsidies to, and/or control over,
private production—as to compromise the essentials of our
private-enterprise system. . . . That risk disappears if aggregate consumer spending, too, is underwritten and maintained at a proper level, one high enough to keep reliance
on supplementary public works within reasonable bounds.[83]

. . . society must not be subject (as it has been subject hith-
erto) to the dilemma of either abandoning the objective of
full employment or else expanding various forms of
planned production to an indefinite extent and in so doing
involuntarily altering the character of the economic system.[84]

Here it seems appropriate to quote from the dust jacket
of *Insuring Full Employment,* published in 1964: "His [Pier-
son's] method is the operational method of science, and
the breakthrough he has achieved lies in the separation of
the economic problem of adequate demand from the political problem of how far to extend the operations of government."

Why Just Consumer Spending Rather Than Total Demand?

Now a little reflection will show that the final market for
purposes of size management has to be the *consumer* market.
Not only is this by far the biggest part of the total—over
60 percent—but private investment ought not to be handled that way in any case; investment needs to be free to
respond to anticipated consumer, government, and foreign
demands in future. And those two other GNP components—government expenditures for goods and services,
and net exports—rule themselves out for equally obvious
reasons. [See sections 8 and 9][85]

That the guarantee of demand should be applied to *consumer* spending rather than to the total of *all* spending on
goods and services (gross national expenditures, equivalent

to GNP) comes about because the other components of total demand just do not lend themselves to this treatment. Nothing is lost, however, since all of the other components would be used to calculate the particular level of consumer spending to be guaranteed.[86]

Perhaps it should be emphasized here that this is not a proposal for more consumption with less investment—surely a dangerous course for our society to take! On the contrary, private investment especially would gain because of the assurance of continuously adequate markets for final products.[87]

Why Not, Then, a Consumer Spending Guarantee Alone?

. . . I have never suggested that full employment could be assured by maintaining, let alone by merely underwriting, only consumption. . . . I strongly emphasized . . . that it would also be essential to underwrite total employment as such, and that the effectuation of this further guarantee would bring into play a second balance wheel—namely, expansions and contractions of public works and services. . . .

I have gone further and warned of the consequences of any attempt to underwrite consumption alone. I will quote this warning . . . at length: "In the first place, the underwriting of aggregate consumer spending would be hard to justify in the absence of an established policy to give jobs on public work projects to persons who might remain involuntarily idle in spite of the inducement afforded to private enterprise by the guarantee. . . . Applied by itself, if such a thing could be imagined, it could involve the government in large expense for consumption subsidies at the very time when men and women were trying in vain to find jobs. This expense would then be challenged as indefensible—with some justice, since it would clearly be better to secure a tangible product in return for the money spent—and the whole policy might under these conditions be condemned as a kind of fiscal sleight of hand." . . .

But, if full employment cannot be guaranteed by underwriting and maintaining private consumption alone, just what is the point of that particular proposal? My answer is: (1) The continuously assured maintenance of a suitably high level of consumer spending would certify that the total market (gross national expenditures) would be large enough to preserve full employment *with resort to supplementary public works and services kept within practical limits*; it would thus make the guaranteeing of full employment itself politically possible. On the other hand, in the absence of such a program with respect to consumption, the volume of public works and services likely at times to be required to preserve full employment would exceed practicable limits—so clearly so that, in our economy, it would not be politically possible, under those conditions, to guarantee full employment. . . . Underwriting consumption and employment—assuring their maintenance at stated levels *in advance*—would have a double advantage: (a) it would provide security and confidence to, and thus tend to sustain the expenditures of, producers and consumers alike; . . . (b) it would obviate undue reliance on, and disputes over, forecasting, by placing the government's compensatory action on an 'if, as, and when' basis dependent on current events as reflected in current operating statistics.[88]

Calculating the Appropriate Level of Consumer Spending

Under EPI there would be a second firm commitment, to a pre-set level of *consumer* spending, with performance monitored by reference to the seasonally adjusted current rate of personal consumption expenditures published quarterly by the Commerce Department. Again it would be a question of holding the figure within a specified range or band rather than on a precise line, and here the band might be, I think, somewhat wider than for employment—say a 2 percent difference between bottom and top, although that again is only a preliminary suggestion, subject to modification in the light of study.[89]

The first step would be to estimate a "full-employment GNP," i.e., to guess as shrewdly as possible the aggregate amount of expenditures for goods and services needed to keep the economy operating at the full-employment level in the year ahead, given the expected rate of price increase (for which, naturally, as low a goal would be set as practicable). Next, estimates would be developed for gross private domestic investment; government spending on goods and services at federal, state, and local levels; and—obviously a minus quality today—net exports. Finally, the necessary (operationally speaking) level of personal consumption expenditures would be derived by subtracting the algebraic sum of those estimated other GNP components from the estimated full-employment GNP. Being the residual number, the consumer spending commitment would accommodate itself to the desired size of the federal government's program; the less government spending intended, the more consumer spending needed, and conversely. And it would accommodate itself too to the state of the trade balance that seemed most likely to develop in the light of circumstances and the foreign policy that our country wanted to follow.[90]

Private investment would still fluctuate, although much less than before, under the conditions of general economic stabilization envisaged here. A technical question would therefore arise as to whether to estimate gross private domestic investment for this purpose at the *level actually expected* in the year ahead—regardless of whether that level is expected to be unusually high, unusually low, or in between—or whether to take it at its *anticipated cyclical-average level*. Either alternative would yield a definite solution having certain advantages and disadvantages.

Probably the choice should lean in the direction of using the cyclical-average level (which amounts nowadays to something like 14 percent of GNP, with investment in residential construction and business inventory changes included). The private-investment swings would then be mostly compensated by means of opposite movements of public works, which would tend to stabilize the construction industry, rather than by means of less convenient opposite movements of the consumer-spending target.[91]

6.

The Consumer Spending Stabilizer

How would consumer spending be held at its guaranteed level? Pierson maintains that there could be numerous options, but all of them would involve the principle that consumer purchasing power would (if or when necessary for honoring the guarantee) be enlarged or reduced by tax or transfer-payment adjustments.

For enlarging it when necessary, Pierson first laid down many years ago the following *general* propositions:

> This could be handled in a variety of ways. Congress would, however, presumably want to consider the following principles in ruling how this should be done. (1) *Adequacy of amount:* the formula selected would have to permit payments to be made to consumers up to a total sufficient to take care of any under-spending likely to arise in a full-employment situation. (2) *Broad and fair distribution:* (a) payments should in general go to the broad ranks of Americans throughout the country, which means in effect that a large part of the total would go to low-income groups. This is necessary for reasons of equity, and it is necessary also in order to keep down the cost to the government, since the low-income groups would spend a larger fraction of these payments and save less. (b) The purpose of maintaining the over-all market should not, however, be subordinated, or normal competitive incentives undermined, by treating the underwriting program as essentially a vehicle for redistribution of income. (c) The distribution should not favor special interest groups. In general, wherever particular groups have a legitimate claim to preferential treatment, such treatment should be accorded by special legislative enactment and not by introducing biases into the program for maintaining the over-all spending level. Any balancing payments required under the latter program should be made available to the general public with a minimum of distinctions between persons. (3) *Flexibility:* the formula would have to contain within itself, as part of the policy laid down by Congress, features enabling the payments to

be started, stopped, expanded, or contracted on short notice (say, each quarter) so as to adapt to changes in the ratio
of consumers' spending out of their regular incomes. (4)
Operating simplicity: the program should not be unduly complicated in administration, and as far as possible it should
use agencies and mechanisms already in operation.[92]

In terms of *specifics,* the following early suggestion of his
may again be of topical interest today:

> The spendings tax . . . can restrict spending to any desired
> extent, both by reducing disposable income and also by
> causing some people to save more of their disposable in-
> come and spend less. It can permit exemptions according
> to family status, and employ the principle of progression
> in accordance with ability to pay. It can be collected along
> with the income tax, thus simplifying the administrative
> problem. Like the income tax, it can in large part be with-
> held at the source on a current or short-interval basis, thus
> allowing the brakes to be applied to consumer spending,
> and again released, without any loss of time.[93]

For the most part, however, Pierson has in recent years
talked about using either (1) a variable income tax or (2)
a variable sales bonus/sales tax to achieve the purpose.

Two Possibilities

> Only two of the possible final-adjustment methods will be
> mentioned here. One would entail raising or lowering
> slightly the withholding rate on the personal income tax,
> after preferably first adding a negative income tax feature
> so as to avoid having to use separate, special devices for
> reaching low-income households. Enough has been written
> about the negative income tax to show that its introduction
> would be feasible. A guaranteed household income plan,
> effectuated through such a negative tax, furthermore de-
> serves consideration as an antipovertry measure—*provided*
> always that full employment be guaranteed too, lest the
> income-guarantee plan perpetuate the division between
> those who can get jobs and those who can't. Under EPI the
> allowances (negative income taxes) would then be raised,
> and the positive income taxes lowered, whenever it was
> necessary to increase consumer spending so as to meet the

guarantee, while the positive income taxes would be raised, and the allowances lowered—although never below their base level—in the opposite case.

Another alternative, first suggested [by Pierson] many years ago, would be to institute a standby two-way federal tax-or-bonus scheme at consumer sales points. Under this plan, when consumer spending was running too low, all buyers of goods and services at retail would receive from the sellers special coupons or stamps. Unlike food stamps, these income-booster coupons would be convertible into cash at a bank or post office if promptly presented. On the other hand, when consumer spending was running too high, the device would become a sales tax, automatically reducing the amount of consumer spending received by business, net of this tax, as much as necessary for purposes of guarantee fulfillment.[94]

Administering the Stabilizer

[The] agency set up to administer fiscal policy in the interest of full-employment stability . . . would be charged by Congress with the continuing duty of expanding or contracting aggregate consumer spending power, in accordance with the law, to the extent that might prove necessary to make actual consumer spending correspond to the guarantees previously given. In short, power would have to be delegated to this agency to make distributions of money, and to suspend, increase, or even impose certain taxes under conditions prescribed by Congress. Congress would determine what formulas should be used for expansion and for contraction. The agency in the executive branch would exercise discretion as to the rates of subsidy or tax required to effectuate the policy.

As the basis for action, the executive agency would compare the current rate of consumer spending, as shown by the series prepared by the Department of Commerce on "consumer expenditures for goods and services" (if that were designated the official series) with the "right" rate, derived by applying appropriate seasonal factors to the guaranteed total for the year. The quarter might be the most convenient unit of time for administrative purposes. . . .

Determination of the proper amount of consumer spending in connection with an underwriting program would be a technical matter, presumably left to the executive branch but under policy directions from Congress, involving a number of considerations . . . (which) have to do with choices between alternative price-level policies, with prospective cost levels, with prospective levels of private capital formation, and with prospective levels of demand on the part of foreigners and the government itself.

A large part of the statistical information suitable for preliminary estimates is provided in the various national income series and related series prepared in the Department of Commerce. In general it may be said that the various statistical estimates that would be required in connection with an underwriting program will have to be made in any case.[95]

A point requiring further analysis, and perhaps some experimentation, is the width of the margin that should be allowed between minimum and maximum levels of aggregate consumer spending. The guarantee should not be so inflexible as to create administrative problems out of all proportion to the gain to be hoped for from elimination of a fractionally small upward pressure on prices. On the other hand, the controlling agency could probably operate quite comfortably with the top limit standing only a very slight percentage above the guaranteed minimum. For example, experience might show that a 2 percent margin was sufficient.[96]

The criteria by which any formula for contracting consumer spending should be judged are essentially the same as the criteria applicable to programs for expanding this spending—namely, adequacy of amount, broad and fair distribution (in this case, distribution of the *deductions* from spending power), flexibility, and operating simplicity. With regard to broad and fair distribution, the plan definitely must restrict the spending of the average man, but, on the other hand, it should be so framed as to avoid regressive features such as are found in the ordinary sales tax.[97]

Three points that are fundamental to this proposal must be kept in mind. . . . (1) The method or methods actually used would depend on the decision of Congress, taken after consideration of the President's recommendations.

(2) The target level also would depend on the decision of Congress. (3) Only a deviation of consumer spending from its predetermined target level—and not ideas or political pressures of the moment—would bring the adjustment mechanism into play.[98]

7.

Implications for Inflation

Inasmuch as the fear of stirring up inflation has been the greatest single deterrent to mounting any strong attack on the unemployment problem, Pierson's contention that it is possible to have full employment without inflation calls for particular attention.

> The weightier reason for caution on full employment is, of course, inflation. Those who believe that reducing unemployment must increase inflation may even conclude that full employment would be a mistake. Or, if uncomfortable with that conclusion or with the underlying trade-off premise or both, they may decide that the two evils have to be attacked simultaneously but by wholly separate means. In point of fact the remedies *are* separate for price rises caused by the oil shortage or by depletion of any other natural resource, but otherwise they are largely the same.[99]

Mostly on the basis of the special features of his EPI proposal, Pierson takes the offensive on the inflation issue.

"Best Cure for Inflation—Guaranteed Full Employment"

> If full employment were, as so often alleged, bound to generate inflation, amending the Employment Act to give it real teeth might have little point. But two recent developments have brought that gloomy thesis into the most serious question—first, the ample demonstration that inflation now tends to occur even without full employment, and second, the not unrelated shift of informed public opinion into favoring an incomes policy of some kind to help maintain price stability. Thus full employment need no longer carry such burdens as do not, properly speaking, belong to it.

> More than that, however, it is here submitted that a program of guaranteed full employment along the lines suggested would not only not feed inflation but actually be the best cure for inflation. This is asserted for two reasons in

combination. First, the ceilings on employment and on consumer spending that would be imposed under this approach would choke off upward demand spirals almost entirely. This is the built-in "mechanical" aspect. It would limit "demand pull" directly, as already emphasized, and indirectly it would also moderate the wage-demand side of the "cost push" by holding down the prices that make up the worker's cost of living. Second, there is the psychological point that cannot be proved but that should appeal to common sense—a point that would arise from the very fact of the government's readiness to commit itself in this unprecedented way. An agreement on the part of the government to assure a total market adequate for business prosperity, and to assure continuous full employment for labor, should be enough to persuade business and labor leaders to agree to abide by some reasonable set of price and wage guidelines.[100]

EPI would also lower unit costs of production in two other ways. Not only does full employment spread the overhead cost over more units of production, but the elimination of business cycles would minimize costs from business and labor efforts to cushion future slumps with special business reserves, job-security clauses in union contracts, etc.[101]

To some extent Pierson's argument rests on his optimistic view of the chances for greater moderation on the price-wage front under a government willing and able to assume its own share of responsibility.

Those who blame inflation on the incurable wickedness of Big Business or Big Labor or both often seem unaware of how far the behavior of both has been caused by the malfunctioning of our economy—its cyclical instability combined with secular weakness—the inevitability of which is precisely what needs to be denied. Once the government stood ready to assure continuously adequate total demand for products and for workers, (1) all business would have more chance to spread their overhead costs and hold prices down; (2) management in areas of administered pricing could logically give up planning for extra profits in boom times to cushion losses in future slumps; and (3) union leaders would feel less pressure to demand extreme hourly wage rates on the one hand, or annual pay guarantees on the other, to fortify their members against the return of unemployment.[102]

The Responsibility Issue

Pierson believes that the Federal Government's acceptance of its due responsibility for the economy "would be a publicly understood signal that business and labor should also accept theirs and agree voluntarily on some fair system of guidance for wages and prices."[103]

> But how can one be confident that an understanding . . . could ever be negotiated with them [the leaders of labor, business, and farmers] . . .? The answer to this seems to me to be relatively simple; *because* the leaders of the major economic interest groups in our society are, by and large, realists. As realists they must know that the vigor with which their constituents look after their own exclusive interests *can* affect the national interest—that it is even possible for excessive demands for pay or profits to impair the viability of our economy. And secondly, any realist is bound to recognize that continuously assured full employment and adequate overall demand would be an unparalleled economic blessing. . . .

> Notice, however, the catch. It would be only the confident expectation of those results, created by the Government's guarantee, that would make it possible to negotiate the understanding. At least I do not myself see much logical or historical reason to suppose that the leaders of labor, business, and farmers would give their pledge in exchange for a mere hope. It seems to come down to this: if the Government in its proper sphere would undertake to assume the necessary degree of responsibility for our economy, why should they not do likewise?[104]

> Once our national government stood ready to accept its due economic responsibility by agreeing to maintain prosperity and guaranteed job opportunity, I suspect that business and labor would also accept theirs by agreeing voluntarily on some fair system of guidance for wages and prices. The reason for thinking that this might happen, when it hasn't in the past, is simply that the chemistry of the situation and of public opinion would be basically altered.[105]

Parenthetically, Pierson carries his "chemistry" argument further than that:

There would thus also arise opportunities to review other basic questions of efficiency and fairness that seldom get a hearing today—e.g., how minimum wages should relate to average wages, and poverty-line supports to minimum wages, and how unions and management can do better justice to all concerned on problems like temporary work and chronic absenteeism.[106]

But, to come back to the main theme,

Industry would be assured of a level of demand adequate to sustain business prosperity indefinitely; labor, of enough jobs to go around. Public opinion, if honestly and thoroughly informed, would recognize that there was no longer any real excuse for anyone's refusal to join in curbing the common enemy, inflation. . . .

In conclusion, for the various reasons cited,

EPI would largely end the inflationary *expectations* from which *current* inflation draws tremendous force today.[107]

Natural Resource Scarcities: a Separate Problem

The oil problem and other natural resource scarcities are open to inventive solutions, too, but would of course remain as a somewhat longer-term part of the price-level question.[108]

A distinction has to be drawn, however, between the upward pressurs on prices that come from the growing scarcities of oil and other non-renewable natural resources and those that derive from other causes. In the former case there is clearly no ready-made answer, so that some rise in the general American price level seems inevitable in the years just ahead. What can help us here is the discovery of substitute materials and, above all, new power-generating methods, capital-saving inventions, conservation and recycling, and more-explicit emphasis on the *qualitative* aspects of economic growth.[109]

The conclusions about inflation that Pierson has elaborated over the years are foreshadowed thus in one of his earliest articles:.

The danger of the wage-price or price-wage spiral has to be faced resolutely and realistically in any case, unless full employment itself is deliberately avoided. A program of underwriting consumer spending should prove a positive asset in this connection, since by judicious management it could be made to yield to the upward pressure just enough to enable it to resist and prevent really serious dislocations. The known existence of a top limit on consumer spending would have publicity value in connection with deliberations concerning the advisability of increases in particular production costs, including collective bargaining conferences to adjust particular money rates of wages. Where increases in such costs appeared in advance to be desirable or inevitable, this would be taken into account in deciding upon the dollar amount of spending to be guaranteed for the ensuing year. In other words, a slight increase in spending and prices could be allowed.[110]

8.

Implications for the Relationship Between the Public and Private Spheres

Pierson's proposal also undertakes to surmount another major barrier to serious efforts to achieve full employment—the fear that such efforts must steadily extend the public sector to a degree unacceptable in a private enterprise system; *the fear*, in short, *of "creeping socialism."* We pick up again here the thread of the argument which was introduced at the beginning of section 5 above.

> The need for expanded activities in the public sector and the need for full employment have become closely entwined in the minds of many people. Economists by and large have now disentwined the two. Nevertheless that unhappy union, existing only in the mind, has long haunted the effort to insure full employment in the United States, and important insights can be gained by a careful examination of it.
>
> Stated in simplest terms, the thought that has caused so much difficulty is this: since there seems to be a sizeable gap between the level of employment that private enterprise—with the addition of normal government operations—is able to maintain and the level of employment corresponding to full employment, extra government activities are evidently needed to fill that gap.[111]
>
> It is . . . said that actually *guaranteeing* full employment would force expansion of the public sector at the private sector's expense, whether intended or not.[112]

Pierson simply denies this, and points out that under his proposal decisions as to the size of the public sector would be made by the public through a democratically elected President and Congress. Any "creeping" toward socialism would have to be deliberate, and done in the open.

This thought that causes the difficulty is rebutted by merely citing again the actual choice that the government has when compensatory action is needed for shorter or longer periods in order to close the employment gap. To repeat, the government has the choice between increasing its own spending for goods and services and increasing the spending for goods and services on the part of the public at large, the latter by means of larger transfer payments or smaller taxes.

It follows that the question of how much the government ought to be spending on public works and services should be decided on its merits. . . . To push for expansion of government operations on the ground that this is the only way to close a persistent employment gap is to confuse the issue and end up by hurting the prospects for full employment.[113]

In deriving the guaranteed consumer spending rate

The key quantity subtracted from the "needed" GNP—along with anticipated private domestic investment, state and local government purchases, and net exports—would be a federal government component made up of items that the President and Congress concluded should be in the budget for their own sake, not just to fill gaps. Although the public jobs throttle would at times still have to be opened or closed a little, because of net error in the various advance estimates, what this approach means is that basically all parts of the full employment not public by choice would be reserved to the private domain.[114]

In point of fact, far from extending the public sector at the expense of private enterprise, Pierson argues that EPI would have a stimulating effect on private investment.

. . . here we see clearly why EPI would strengthen the private-enterprise market system. Last-resort government jobs would not threaten to have to grow and grow, since EPI would assure manufacturers, farmers and other producers of goods and services *that they would always have a big enough market to compete for.* The federal government's demand—used, as just explained, in calculating the to-be-guaranteed consumer demand—would include all of the items wanted by the President and Congress for their own

sake, but not any others. . . . We could therefore always
have the GNP level we need without having a public sector
level that we as a nation don't want.[115]

. . . the method of determining the consumer spending
guarantee—by having all items wanted by the President
and Congress for their own sake, but not any others, included in the subtotal *subtracted* from the estimated necessary GNP to arrive at that—would be altogether favorable
to private producers. For it would certify that all parts of
the full employment not public by deliberate choice would
be reserved to the private domain. . . . The Gordian knot
that has seemed to tie promises of full employment to
threats of bigger and bigger government would be effectively cut.[116]

In the first place such an appproach would emphasize individual consumer choice and sovereignty, which is another
way of saying that it would let consumers buy all the goods
and services that our economy could produce for them,
after taking care of genuine investment needs, and would
let them decide by their own preferences what kinds of
goods and services ought to be produced in greater quan-
tities. . . .

In the second place, the approach by way of guaranteed
consumer spending would hold definite advantages for the
businessman and the farmer. The potential stimulus to the
retailer and producer of consumer goods is particularly
obvious. But the effect would not end there; the producer
of capital goods should also derive some benefit. For example, a manufacturer considering whether or not to buy
new equipment would be aware that the market in which
the products from that equipment would be sold would not
be subject to periodic collapse for reasons of general un-
derspending. Hence he would tend to go ahead, if other
circumstances were favorable, and place his order with the
maker of the equipment. . . .

A third advantage of the underwriting technique, applied
to the over-all consumer market, would be that it would
maintain the conditions in which competition would have
all the scope possible under modern conditions of mass
production. Unlike the proposals sometimes advanced for
establishing and underwriting quotas for particular indus-

tries or particular producers, it would refrain from guaranteeing anything to any particular industry or producer but instead would assure private enterprise that full-employment levels of production would return a fair profit when averaged over the whole. Thus it would encourage flexibility rather than promote industry-by-industry stratification.[117]

Also important, although less basic than the fear that guaranteed full employment must expand the public sector, has been the fear that it necessarily implies *continual budget deficits*. To this Pierson replies that under EPI deficits would be neither inevitable nor unsound; and indeed he points out they obviously occur when unemployment is heavy too. [His further argument that guaranteed full employment could indirectly do exactly the opposite, i.e., form the basis for *solving* the current deficit problem, is linked to international considerations and is therefore dealt with in the next section.]

> One of the most controversial questions in the debate over full employment is this: Will not a full-employment program involve a continuous and disastrous series of deficits in the Federal budget? Some opponents of full employment not only say that it will and must involve continuing deficits, but also say that we cannot stand these unbalanced budgets and therefore cannot afford full employment. . . .
>
> The approach we are considering here . . . assumes two things: first, that, if the objective of full employment and the objective of a balanced budget come into conflict, it is the balanced budget that must for the time give way; and second, that firm and intelligent action must be taken to rectify more and more those things that so unbalance our economy as to make full employment and a balanced budget likely to be incompatible. As you can see, this second point presupposes the view that full employment will not, in the first instance, normally bring a balanced budget—that it will not tend to do so until we, ourselves, do something about such things as excessive inequality of income, monopolistic restrictions, and several other very troublesome problems. I may say that, in my opinion, we would overlook this obligation at our peril.[118]

It is often said that we can't afford the unbalanced budgets. But this puts the blame for deficits in the wrong place. The real villain of the piece, if deficit financing is required, is the too-little spending or oversaving tendency, not the full-employment policy. For, in the absence of a full-employment policy, the budget will be unbalanced anyway by shrinking tax revenues and growing relief handouts.[119]

In other words, balancing the budget would not be a real alternative at all. Trying to balance it would, in those circumstances, be perfectly futile, and a demand that it be done would be a cliché, the propitiation of a demon who doesn't inhabit the cave any more, a gesture which everyone understands is purely ceremonial.[120]

The ability to maintain full employment presupposes freedom to lower taxes or increase government outlays when the economy needs an additional lift, and to raise taxes or reduce government outlays in the face of a threat of inflationary overspending or overfull employment.

Such fiscal action is bound to cause budget deficits some of the time. There is no getting around that point. The choice simply has to be made between maintaining full employment and trying at all times to balance the budget.

This choice, however, would be a fairly easy one even if unemployment were not as costly and damaging to the nation as it is. Such budget deficits cannot be shown to be either irresponsible or harmful to our economic system if they are incurred only when an honest effort is also being made to maintain full employment as far as possible by other, basic means. Moreover, in those conditions in which such fiscal action unbalances the budget, a failure to act would also (passively or unintentionally) unbalance it . . . by reducing tax revenues and forcing an increase in relief expenditures. This is a crucial point.[121]

Thus the issue as to the appropriate proportions between public and private investment in our economy brings to the fore a theme emphasized by Pierson throughout his many publications—namely, the useful distinction between *"basic"* and *"compensatory"* policies.

This question may be clarified further by emphasizing a

distinction between basic policies on the one hand and compensatory fiscal policies on the other. The role of basic policies, in the approach under discussion, is to minimize reliance on compensatory policies that will usually occasion budget deficits to prevent deflation and unemployment or else may involve last-minute, emergency action against a threatened inflation. The role of compensatory fiscal policies is to provide further support and flexibility as needed, to the end that assurance can be given that full employment will be maintained without inflation, irrespective of how sufficient or insufficient the basic policies currently in operation may be for that purpose.

A commitment is therefore given that compenatory policies will be used if necessary to prevent over-all deflation, or to prevent over-all inflation. But at the same time basic policies are pressed vigorously—i.e. policies, of whatever kind, that will minimize long-run deflationary tendencies—not forgetting measures to prevent speculation and localized inflation from getting started and thus setting the stage for a violent tendency toward deflationary reaction at a later period. In this context, obviously, the question asked about any basic measure that may be proposed is not "how much additional employment, if any, will result if basic policy X is adopted?" but rather, "Will the deficit or other difficulty associated with maintenance of full employment become smaller if basic policy X is adopted?"[122]

Assured full employment calls partly for basic or long-run government policies that are not supposed to be changed from moment to moment just because some economic barometer happens to be rising or falling, and partly for compensatory policies that are resorted to when necessary to close up any remaining gaps. . . .

Long-run or basic policies are, one can easily sense, the foundation. Although they must serve a variety of strength and welfare aims of which full employment is only one, they should certainly as far as practicable be framed with an eye to serving that. In other words, they should reinforce the self-sustaining qualities of our economy, so as to reduce the need to resort to special, compensatory measures to prevent deflation and inflation.

On the supply side, it is basic and particularly important

to enforce price competition where feasible and, beyond that, restrain monopolistic and oligopolistic price demands; to establish as a guiding principle in collective bargaining that wage increases cannot disregard certain limits (not always easy to identify in practice, of course) imposed by productivity increases; and to remove various imperfections and rigidities in the labor market, especially by creating greater labor mobility through an expansion of training, retraining, and job-counseling services.

On the demand side, it is necessary to maintain mass purchasing power—for example, by high wages (subject to the qualification just given), a strong social-security system which on balance is paying out rather than accumulating funds, and a progressive tax structure. At the same time it is also necessary to maintain business-investment incentives.

To the extent that these two aims come into conflict—and the existence of some conflict here can hardly be denied—as constructive a compromise as possible needs to be worked out.

There is evidently nothing wrong with correct basic policies as the final answer to full employment except that they suffer from the following limitations: The possibility of envisaging all the economic consequences of a given basic policy action has its limits. Our ability to agree among ourselves on just what action is basically needed or wanted is practically nonexistent. The factors in the world situation that are not under legislative control will not stand still!

That is to say, wise basic policies can be accepted as only part of the answer to full employment. They must try to give as good a first approximation as possible, but additional measures will be needed to complete the job.[123]

In *my* view of our national priorities, much larger expenditures are clearly needed—by government and business both—for the environment, housing, mass transit, other city services, health, education, backward rural areas, and so on. Meeting those social needs would also provide more jobs per dollar, and more useful ones, than other kinds of expansion could.

Yet to say that some particular program along these lines is essential to get full employment as a by-product is, I am sure, simply wrong. Congress might settle for a less liberal policy than the President had recommended; but the super-priority, full employment, would be achieved all the same—under my proposals—only with a somewhat different job mix.[124]

9.

Implications for International Relations

While familiar at first hand with some aspects of American foreign policy, and certainly aware that influences between domestic and international policy run in both directions, Pierson has always strongly maintained that emphasis in the economic sphere should be placed on the former. The opening paragraphs of his earliest book threw down the gauntlet:

> The crux of a sound policy for the United States is the knowledge that domestic economic measures and domestic economic measures alone can bring permanent prosperity and full employment. Many are inclined to say that sound domestic policy is one thing and sound foreign policy another. But in the long run the latter is impossible without the former.

> The two halves of this thesis both deserve the closest scrutiny. First, that the United States can have lasting and guaranteed full employment without resorting to external expansion or aggression in any shape or form, if the American people will understand the conditions making that possible and will insist upon having them. Second, that lasting and guaranteed full employment can never be achieved by means of a conventionally vigorous economic foreign policy—which at best can make temporary jobs, probably for the most part in munitions plants or with the nation's armed forces.[125]

The main binding element here is obviously foreign trade. The key point in Pierson's position about foreign trade is that it should be used for lowering costs and raising levels of living (the comparative advantages principle) but should *not* be used as a crutch for the over-all level of domestic employment. Yet a crutch is what it often is treated as being, and that approach will never be abandoned in the absence of an employment guarantee, as under EPI.

... expanded foreign trade does not need to be justified as a means of increasing domestic employment. It is fully justified and required on other grounds. Assuming it is brought about in a situation in which trade barriers and discriminations are at a reasonable minimum, so that advantage can be taken of regional specialization in accordance with comparative efficiencies of production, expanded foreign trade should make a striking contribution to international harmony and security and to higher standards of living here and abroad. . . .

Turning the relationship around, a sound domestic program for full employment is the best guarantor of expanded foreign trade . . . a sound domestic program for full employment, founded on internal measures and not dependent on export surpluses, will create among American businessmen, workers, and farmers the conditions and the psychology on which broad American support for liberal trading practice must ultimately rest.[126]

Pierson repeatedly emphasizes that *"The Achilles heel of modern capitalism is the constant threat of a shortage of markets."*[127]

Years ago when the ITO—International Trade Organization—charter was being negotiated, . . . my colleagues from the State Department . . . could think of nothing except lowering trade barriers. . . . All the other major countries—in this case the western industrialized countries—said: we don't care so much about that; what we want to know is, are you going to have full employment in the United States, so that you will keep up the demand for our goods?

More recently, and in a more sophisticated form, you get the same thing over and over in the economic committee of the United Nations General Assembly, and in the summer debates of the Economic and Social Council in Geneva. The reasoning is absolutely correct, in my opinion. The less developed countries by and large are never going to be able to develop unless they are allowed to export manufactures—after, of course, first learning to produce manufactures efficiently. The cards are stacked against the possibility of their ever developing strictly as agricultural nations or exporters of raw materials.

Now we in the United States have in recent years spoken very sympathetically of that desire on their part. We have tried to urge our friends in Europe to relax their trade barriers, and successive administrations have tried to get us to lower our own barriers sufficiently. But there have been limits set by the fear of a shortage of markets.[128]

The fundamental point about trade is that our ability to keep our economy running at the full-employment level makes us often try to cure this internal weakness of ours at the expense of other countries; that is, by restricting their exports to us and pushing our exports to them unduly hard. This reflex action manifests the perennial and universal capitalist fear of a shortage of markets. We certainly didn't invent it. In a great country like ours, however, with our worldwide responsibilities, that fear can and should be relieved by domestic means.[129]

EPI, Pierson argues, Would Encourage Liberal Trade Policies and Hold Protectionism in Check

A striking . . . feature of EPI is the way it would help to liberalize foreign trade by ending the historic fear of a shortage of markets, which is the main thing enabling protectionist interests to gain governmental support for trade restrictions.[130]

The ability to maintain full employment by domestic adjustments, regardless of the state of the foreign trade balance, is the first prerequisite for securing a continuously ample volume of a country's foreign trade in general and, in particular, the relaxation of trade restrictions, with resulting enhancement of world security and benefit to the domestic standard of living through encouragement to worthwhile international specialization. A nation liable to depressions is sooner or later bound to adopt illiberal foreign policies such as high tariffs, export subsidies, harsh immigration laws, exploitation (if the nation is powerful) of low-cost foreign sources of raw materials, and aggressive currency devaluation, since these expedients promise to secure additional markets and additional employment opportunity for the domestic population.[131]

In short, Pierson considers that any fundamental improvement in America's international policies and international relations will require paying attention to the central domestic economic problem and solving it, as by adopting the EPI technique. As was noted earlier, his argument is *not* that the rest of the world should also adopt the EPI proposal—even though he has recently conceded that it might work in some other advanced economies too.[132]

> ... the advantages of guaranteed full employment would be not only domestic but international as well. This follows from the fact that our foreign trade balance would logically be one of the factors (one of the components of GNP) to be taken into account in estimating how much consumer spending was required to arrive at a basically adequate total demand for domestic output as a whole.[133]

> ... under EPI the size of the consumer-spending guarantee would automatically rise, other things equal, if an export surplus were expected to decline or an import surplus grow.[134]

> Hence we would be equally able to maintain full employment with an export surplus or an import surplus. Freed from any compulsive, economic-self-defense need to force our exports abroad or stop imports from coming in, we could begin to use our economic foreign policy much less as a weapon and more as an instrument of good will than we have in the past.[135]

> ... the present situation in which the United States (like most other nations) intensifies its pursuit of export markets and its resistance to imports whenever its domestic market shrinks would become obsolete. For ... we could consciously adjust the size of our domestic market, via the consumer spending guarantee, to whatever export or import surplus seemed indicated on broadest policy grounds. In a word, our trade policies would no longer need to be governed by the historic fear of a shortage of markets, and we could wear our good-neighbor face more often.[136]

The basic solution lies in the bold step, not yet tried but feasible, of turning the whole approach completely around. Instead of looking to foreign markets to make up for deficient domestic markets, *guarantee* a domestic consumer market that will be adequate in combination with the expected (net) foreign market, private domestic investment and government demand, and *guarantee* full employment too, using some equally convenient statistical definition.[137]

EPI Would Benefit the Nations of the Third World

... in tomorrow's world, we need to be able to maintain full employment and ample markets for our producers regardless of whether we have an export surplus or not. As a matter of fact, as we grow more mature we ought to act like a mature creditor country and accept an import surplus eventually. Today we have the problems of trade and aid. In the immediate present we need especially to extend aid, more aid than we have been extending to ... less developed countries. If we had achieved continuously assured prosperity we wouldn't need to feel that we couldn't afford to do it. We wouldn't need to feel that we were helping somebody in Asia at the expense of some poor people in Appalachia, because it would be obvious that we could do both.[138]

Internationally, that extra wealth [resulting from full employment] would confirm our ability to extend more generous aid to the world's less developed countries. More (and more fundamental) than that, confidence in our ability to maintain a market adequate for our own full-employment prosperity through domestic policy would substantially deflate our fear of imports and our exaggerated preoccupation with export markets and export surpluses; thus it would enable us to be a "good neighbor" that encourages and helps the less developed countries to shift "from aid to trade" as they become ready for it.[139]

Consequently Pierson makes the point that EPI might even gain us an indispensable ally *in the cause of peace.*

Several decades ago he was thinking of the menace of Soviet hostility mainly from the standpoint of the competition of the two rival systems for the "minds of men."

... The Russians say that recurring depression is inherent in the very fabric and "laws of motion" of our capitalist economy. We know how this assertion is used for propaganda purposes. We also know that it is part of the long-standing, basic Marxist text. We perhaps do not know how firmly the Kremlin now holds this belief, but, above all, what we are not yet in a position to assert conclusively is that the belief is wrong. This is unfortunate because, all other difficulties aside, it is evidently a massive barrier against coming to a satisfactory understanding with Russia and laying the basis for genuine and lasting peace.[140]

Now that it is later in the day, and we all have to consider how to avoid atomic annihilation, Pierson has shifted his emphasis—but not his recommendation:

> It is probable that a satisfactory overall domestic economic policy, centered on continuously assured full employment without inflation—a policy that America could adopt without asking anyone else's permission—would have international repercussions that in turn would give us our best chance of bringing the'deficit to heel. And if that is so, then it is time to take a more hopeful and imaginative look at the chances of reaching agreement with the Russians on instituting a verifiable freeze on the production of atomic weapons and on following that with the progressive scrapping of those already produced, and with other disarmament measures.
>
> One conceivable way to get an agreement—the approach that is apparently being tested now—is to force the Russians into it by our superior strength. To this writer, that notion seems utterly fantastic. Another way of going about it is to keep pressing the Russians for more bilateral talks. That indeed we must do; yet it seems to be an insufficiently promising course of action in view of the mutual distrust.
>
> Why not then choose a broader approach, one that would certainly include the bilateral talks but that would also seek to break the deadlock by bringing nearly the whole weight of Third World opinion to bear in favor of world disarmament? Most of the Third World countries would back a clear-cut disarmament campaign waged by us if they were really our friends. And they would become our real friends if we were a real friend to them—if our "good neighbor" policy were a living reality instead of a half-forgotten slogan.
>
> The touchstone there would be our categorical ability and willingness to help them to grow through trade and (al-

though less fundamentally) through aid. That, however, can only happen after we become able to be sure to keep ourselves prosperous and fully employed without restricting our imports and forcing our exports (weapons included) in the effort to obtain more ample markets. There is the catch.

In other words, what we need to do—not only for obvious domestic reasons but to resume our world leadership, maximize the disarmament probabilities, and in that process also cure our budget deficit—is to guarantee both an adequate level of jobs as such (full employment) and an overall market for goods and services large enough to keep on motivating the requisite amount of production.[141]

The references here to budget deficits, so dominant a topic in economic policy discussions today, are worth noting. On the heels of the "revolution of rising expectations" in the less-developed countries comes a revolt against lowering *established* expectations, centered this time in wealthy countries of the free world caught up in the arms race. When the U.S., for example, insists on having more "guns" but does not agree to pay the price by giving up its accustomed "butter," huge chronic deficits are inevitable. Pierson, at least, is not one who considers that the problem of the deficit can be cured *without* disarmament agreements.

. . . the main cause of those huge deficits is our country's absolute need for an adequate national defense. . . . The heart of the deficit problem is our present continuing need to spend staggeringly large sums on the arms race.[142]

Coming back to economic foreign policy in general, and Pierson's view about how it ought to operate—

If . . . the aim has come to be economic development for all; and if, furthermore, it is true that in many respects the era of international advantage-taking has ended and has been replaced by an era in which international cooperation is fundamental—then it would seem that a pointed analogy should be drawn. Most people recognize that, in interpersonal relations, the insecure person is the one who is continually trying to solve his problems at the expense of others. What seems to need saying is that a powerful but insecure economy would seek to gain markets (involuntarily, so to speak, and to its own regret) at the expense of other economies, whereas a mature and secure economy would be able to provide enough markets for itself without depriving other economies.[143]

10.
How It Can be Done

Pierson contends that Economic Performance Insurance could be quickly introduced once Congress decided to commit itself to full employment. The key legislative action required would be the amending of an already existing general or enabling law.* In addition, most of the administrative machinery for operation of the program is already in place. Consequently, he maintains, since it is unnecessary to wait for full economic recovery before introducing the process with the commitments it involves, guaranteed full employment is a realistic and practical goal for *today*; no need to wait.

On the issue as to whether the operations called for under EPI could be carried out, Pierson writes: "Would the plan work in practice? This final question, to be sure, is not resolvable in advance of an actual trial; probability is the most that can be claimed. Given the various kinds of 'leeway' the plan envisages, I do think that that probability will be found to exist."[146]

Legislative Action

> ... the Employment Act should be amended to assign to Congress an authority—and above all a responsibility—which the original language of the Act fails to give.[147]

> Under that Employment Act of 1946 [as amended by the Full Employment and Balanced Growth Act of 1978] the President's annual Economic Report, with his recommendations for action, is referred to the Joint Economic Com-

---

* In an article which was printed in the *Congressional Record* in 1972 Pierson himself suggested minimum essential language for amending the original Employment Act of 1946.[144] Subsequent passage of the Humphrey-Hawkins bill (Full Employment and Balance Growth Act of 1978) may have considerably complicated the drafting problem, but certainly without affecting any of the principles involved. In his 1977 testimony on that bill, Pierson also suggested possible language for the required minor amendment of the Congressional Budget Act of 1974 which is referred to below.[145]

mittee of Congress. The Committee studies this and issues its own report on it. But then the whole process breaks down. Congress is not obliged to act on the matter in any concerted way. The Committee's report simply goes to the other interested committees of Congress to use as they may see fit. The economic stabilization thrust, no matter how good, is dispersed in thin air.

What is clearly called for is an amendment requiring Congress as a whole to take certain definite decisions by joint or concurrent resolution. Congress should each year either accept or modify the minimum and maximum employment limits and consumer spending limits that would be proposed by the President. Second, it should ask the President to hold total jobs and total consumer spending within those approved limits. Third, it should specify the standby measures—the kinds of public works and services, and of consumer taxes or transfer payments—to be used when and if found needed for a final adjustment. Then the Executive Branch, without interference, should execute the decisions of Congress on the President's original recommendations.[148]

[Thus] two kinds of legislative action are required, the first being new permanent legislation to amend the present law. Permanent legislation could obviously not bind future Congresses on questions of specific *substance,* but it would, as does the Congressional Budget Act of 1974, call on future Congresses to follow certain specific *procedures.*

Incidentally, it would need to amend Section 301 of that Budget Act, which might otherwise be held to prevent authorization of *contingent* modifications of budget outlay and revenue totals as required for maintaining guaranteed levels of employment and consumer spending. The Budget Act pointedly avoids requiring budget *balance* in any given year, and should equally clearly not push the idea of advance budget *rigidity* to the point where that would prevent the maintenance of full employment. A drafting amendment is, therefore, required, to indicate that modifications in the pre-set annual outlay and revenue totals called for under the budget law would be permissible, if specifically occasioned by last-resort actions needed to honor the commitments under the employment law. With that change made, neither act would contravene the other.[149]

Note again that, under the EPI proposal, the decisions finally reached on numerical limits and on methods of enforcement would be binding decisions. Congress would not be giving the President *discretionary* authority for dealing with economic fluctuations. On the contrary, while final-balancing operations, when required, would be conducted by the Executive Branch without further Congressional intervention, resort to those operations would be *mandatory* to honor the specific promises given by Congress and would be precluded in other circumstances.

Objection might be raised to having Congress exercise this authority, binding upon the President. If so, then a procedure involving the opportunity for Presidential vetoes and Congressional overrides could be used instead, although a testing of the Constitutional question raised by such an objection might be welcomed first. What is essential, however, is simply that, under EPI, the annual process of setting the stage for the next economic year would have to end with definite, unambiguous decisions on the lower and upper limits to the guarantees, and on the standby methods for use in enforcing those limits.

The regular committee system of Congress would meanwhile deal with authorizations and appropriations as it does now. For example, tax reforms shaped by the Senate Finance Committee or by Ways and Means would not clash with the standby tax adjustment mechanism, but would only affect (by altering after-tax income and its distribution) the likelihood that those mechanisms would have to be called ito play.[150]

Operational Procedures

Once adopted, the new employment law would have the President each year recommend in his Economic Report (1) lower and upper limits to employment and consumer-spending guarantees for the year ahead [and possibly also, Pierson notes elsewhere, for half-yearly or even quarterly periods during the transition to full employment], and (2) contingent or standby measures for the adjustment of both magnitudes, as already explained. Congress would then each year have its Joint Economic Committee analyze those recommendations, and would after that follow a procedure leading to a concurrent resolution setting forth its own decisions on those same points.

To illustrate, suppose that these procedures had been in effect for the year 1977, when unemployment averaged 7 percent, civilian employment averaged 90.55 million persons, the GNP was $1887 billion and consumer spending came to $1207 billion. *If* the President had been in a position to propose a 3.5 percent limit to unemployment instead, he would have recommended holding employment, say, between 94 and 95 million and—I here arbitrarily assume $50 billion added to GNP for each percentage point subtracted from unemployment—holding consumer spending between $1320 and $1345 billion (based on an estimated full-employment GNP of $2062 billion). And *if* Congress had then decided on a tighter definition of full employment, say 3 percent unemployment, but a smaller government program and hence an offsetting, larger amount of consumer spending, the guarantee figures as modified by Congress would have been: employment $94.5-95.5 million and consumer spending, e.g., $1360-$1385 billion.[151]

None of this, however, invalidates the point that standby authority would be needed to take care of possible developments not foreseen early in the year. To maintain full employment and avoid overfull employment, as officially defined and as measured by the officially designated statistical series, it would often be necessary before the year was over to raise or lower the expenditure on public works and services rather than hold to any particular level that might have been indicated in the beginning. In case of an increase, the regular program would then be exceeded.

True, the pegging of consumer expenditures ought to yield a *good first approximation* of full employment, at the originally authorized level of government expenditures for goods and services. This is the basic purpose of that maneuver. But it is essential for an understanding of my proposal to recognize that no more than that is claimed. The various calculations would not be expected to be perfectly "correct" except by accident.

The export [or import] surplus might turn out to be somewhat larger or smaller than anticipated. So might private gross capital expenditures. So might government purchases of goods and services at State and local levels; these, of course, lie largely outside of Federal control, and might begin to move less predictably than they have in the past.

71

So might the "pull" exerted by the demand for goods and services on the level of employment be somewhat larger or smaller than anticipated, since the price-level trend and the rate of introduction of labor-saving processes might both differ from what was expected. If various monopolistic elements in the economy were stronger than foreseen, for example, and competitive elements weaker, a given total of effective demand would yield somewhat less production than expected, and somewhat higher prices.

It is not, however, that these discrepancies would do any harm. Barring an actual breakdown on the price-stabilization front, they would not. A high degree of precision is not essential. Perhaps I should stress that unlimited faith in the GNP system of measurement is not essential either under this suggested procedure, which would employ that system as a scaffolding which is very useful in approaching the problem in hand but is discarded after it had served its purpose. Whenever the several original estimating errors came close to offsetting each other, employment would in fact tend to remain between floor and ceiling levels without compensatory expansion or contraction of public works. At other times, some compensatory public-works expansion or contraction would be called for.[152]

A special unit, most likely in the Labor Department, would be charged with initiating action to raise or lower employment, and one in the Treasury Department (or possibly a joint task force of IRS, HEW and CEA?) with triggering additions to or subtractions from consumer spending. These experts would need good judgment for solving problems of timing. One group would be working with preliminary tabulations of employment data due to be published about three weeks after the period to which they applied; the other, with data on consumption expenditures for which the Commerce Department publishes preliminary figures some three weeks after the end of each quarter. Both would obviously have to keep close watch on a wide array of forecasts for individual industries and on other relevant economic data.

Although statistical leads and lags would be much less troublesome in the absence of business cycles than they are today, very real technical difficulties would remain, both in knowing the facts and in getting operational decisions carried out. Since the mandate would be to stay within designated bands or ranges, corrections would commonly have to be introduced on an anticipatory basis. Postponing action until either indicator was already too low or too high would breach the continuity of the pattern before correction could take hold. Again, once correction did take hold, how soon should action be terminated?

Yet there seems no reason to doubt that these problems could be solved. Firstly, the President and Congress would already have weighed the extent of these operating difficulties in deciding how wide the employment and consumer spending bands ought to be. Secondly, Congress might very well agree that employment and consumer spending could, without any presumption of mismanagement, stray outside their "allowable" bands briefly—say for two or three monthly periods or one quarterly period. Finally, as said earlier, a major undertaking would build up both an adequate reserve shelf of last-resort jobs and the capacity of local agencies to act quickly in starting and stopping those job programs once the signal was given. And the essential local cooperation would also be prearranged for quickly activating the consumer spending adjustments.[153]

In implementing EPI a certain number of technical (statistical and economic) studies would obviously need to be made. None of them should prove unduly difficult or time-consuming if tackled with the staff resources available to the President's Council of Economic Advisers and/or the several interested committees of Congress (Joint Economic Committee, Congressional Budget Office, etc.).

One quantitative study that would claim high priority, to get the assurances started off on a realistic basis, would be an assessment of the various stages envisaged leading up from present recession to full employment. Special emphasis would need to be given to estimating an optimum quarter-by-quarter succession of employment and consumer spending levels (the latter calculated, of course, in the context of overall demand or GNP projections). This study would probably follow the common practice of spelling out the considerations for and against faster and slower alternatives, so that informed policy choices could then be made.[154]

Another preparatory step of major importance would be the holding of discussions on anti-inflation policy with representatives of business and labor. As already noted, price spirals would be checked, under EPI, by having ceilings on employment and on consumer spending. In addition to those controls on the "demand pull," however, something should be done to moderate the "cost push" pressures toward higher prices. Much would be accomplished here if the government's own assumption of new responsibility for the economy were matched by business and labor commitments to support a reasonable set of price and wage guidelines. Talks looking to such undertakings by business and labor should be started while the new full-employment legislation was still under debate.[155]

We . . . cannot go from heavy unemployment to full employment overnight; but we *could* immediately set firm performance targets that would get us ahead step by step—quarter by quarter. Then . . . by adopting the insurance approach, we would benefit immediately from all the effects on expectations. This is why we might reach full employment sooner than most of the experts have said we can.[156]

References

1. *Full Employment Without Inflation. Papers on the Economic Performance Insurance (EPI) Proposal,* Allanheld, Osmun & Co., Montclair, New Jersey, 1980, (cited hereafter as FEWI), p. 4. This paper (FEWI, pp. 1-15) appeared first in abridged form in the *Journal of Post Keynesian Economics,* Summer 1979 issue.
2. Opening sentence of an address delivered in 1967, included in *Essays on Full Employment, 1942-1972,* The Scarecrow Press, Inc., Metuchen, New Jersey, 1972 (cited hereafter as *Essays*), p. 277.
3. *Essays,* p. iii.
4. Personal correspondence.
5. FEWI, p. 19. (1978)
6. *Greenwich News,* Dec. 8, 1983, p. 19.
7. *Monterey Peninsula Herald,* March 4, 1970. (Also in FEWI, p. 96.)
8. FEWI, pp. 2-3.
9. *Connecticut Newspapers,* February 20, 1983, p. B4.
10. FEWI, p. 2.
11. *Monterey Peninsula Herald, loc. cit.*
12. *Ibid.*
13. FEWI, p. 3.
14. *Insuring Full Employment. A United States Policy for Domestic Prosperity and World Development,* The Viking Press, New York, 1964, (cited hereafter as IFE), p. 16.
15. FEWI, p. 19. (1978)
16. IFE, p. 16.
17. FEWI, p. 2.
18. *Monterey Peninsula Herald, loc cit.*
19. *Connecticut Newspapers, loc. cit.*
20. FEWI, p. 19. (1978)
21. *Monterey Peninsula Herald,* March 5, 1970. (FEWI, p. 97).
22. *Greenwich News, loc. cit.*
23. FEWI, p. 23. (1978)
24. FEWI, p. 3. Pierson cites Professor Emile Benoit as having particularly emphasized this connection.
25. *Connecticut Newspapers, loc. cit.*
26. *Christian Science Monitor,* July 23, 1949. (FEWI, p. 154).
27. FEWI, p. 18. (1978) Last two italics added.
28. *Commercial and Financial Chronicle,* May 8, 1969. (FEWI, p. 107.)
29. *Ibid.* (FEWI, pp. 109-110.)
30. FEWI, p. 4.
31. IFE, pp. 5-6.
32. FEWI, pp. 4-5.
33. *Essays,* pp. iii-iv.
34. *Connecticut Newspapers, loc. cit.*
35. IFE, p. 6.
36. FEWI, p. x.
37. FEWI, p. 38. (1977)
38. *Connecticut Newspapers, loc. cit.* Italics added.
39. *Ibid.*
40. *Monterey Peninsula Herald,* March 2, 1970. (FEWI, pp. 91-92.) Italics added.
41. FEWI, p. x.
42. FEWI, p. 13.
43. IFE, pp. 85-86. (FEWI, p. 122.)
44. *Full Employment,* Yale University Press, New Haven, 1941, (cited hereafter as FE), pp. 60-61.
45. Personal correspondence.
46. FE, p. 10.
47. FEWI, p. 16. (1978)
48. FEWI, p. 5.
49. *Full Employment and Free Enterprise,* Public Affairs Press, Washington, D.C., 1947, p. v.
50. FEWI, p. 16. (1978)
51. FEWI, p. 21. (1978)
52. FE, p. 256.
53. FEWI, p. 16. (1978)
54. FEWI, p. 34. (1977)
55. FEWI, p. 5.
56. *Connecticut Newspapers, loc cit.*
57. FEWI, p. 35. (1977)
58. IFE, p. 86. (FEWI, p. 122.)
59. *Commercial and Financial Chronicle, loc. cit.* (FEWI, p. 113.)
60. FEWI, pp. 36 and 41. (1977. The quoted summary appeared originally in the *Congressional Record* for July 26, 1976.)
61. IFE, pp. 100-101.
62. *Congressional Record,* March 1, 1972. (FEWI, pp. 71-72.)
63. *Honolulu Advertiser,* August 14, 1971. (FEWI, p. 80.)
64. *Congressional Record, loc. cit.*
65. IFE, p. 122.
66. FEWI, p. 2.
67. FEWI, p. 101. (1970)
68. *Congressional Record, loc. cit.*
69. IFE, p. 122.
70. IFE, pp. 123-124.
71. *Congressional Record, loc. cit.*

72. FEWI, p. 6.
73. FEWI, p. ix.
74. FEWI, p. 1.
75. FEWI, pp. 101-102. (1970)
76. *Fiscal Policy for Full Employment*, National Planning Association Planning Pamphlets No. 45, May 1945. (*Essays*, p. 124.)
77. *American Economic Review*, March 1944. (FEWI, p. 202).
78. FEWI, pp. 8-9. Italics added.
79. Radio broadcast, February 1975. (FEWI, pp. 53-54.)
80. *Review of Economics and Statistics*, August 1949. (FEWI, p. 138.)
81. Radio broadcast, *loc. cit.*
82. Paper presented to Institute on Postwar Rconstruction, New York University, December 19, 1945. (FEWI, p. 157).
83. *American Economic Review*, September 1955. (FEWI, p. 124.)
84. FE, p. 24.
85. Radio broadcast, *loc. cit.*
86. FEWI, p. 22. (1978)
87. *Connecticut Newspapers*, *loc. cit.*
88. *Review of Economics and Statistics*, *loc. cit.* (FEWI, pp. 137-138.)
89. FEWI, p. 6.
90. FEWI, p. 7.
91. IFE, pp. 41-42. Italics added.
92. *American Economic Review*, March 1944. (FEWI, p. 195.)
93. *Ibid.* (FEWI, p. 201.)
94. FEWI, p. 9.
95. *American Economic Review*, March 1944. (FEWI, pp. 203-204.)
96. *Ibid.* (FEWI, p. 201.)
97. *Ibid.* (FEWI, pp. 200-201.)
98. IFE, p. 40.
99. FEWI, p. x.
100. *Congressional Record*, *loc. cit.* (FEWI, pp. 78-79.)
101. FEWI, p. 12.
102. *Congressional Record*, *loc. cit.* (FEWI, p. 79.)
103. FEWI, p. 26. (1977)
104. *Commercial and Financial Chronicle*, *loc. cit.* (FEWI, p. 110.)
105. FEWI, p. 23. (1978)
106. FEWI, pp. 12-13.
107. *Ibid.*
108. FEWI, p. 17. (1978)
109. FEWI, pp. 22. (1978)
110. *American Economic Review*, March 1944. (FEWI, p. 208.)
111. IFE, p. 146.
112. FEWI, p. 35. (1977)
113. IFE, p. 147.
114. FEWI, p. 35. (1977)
115. FEWI, p. 22. (1978)
116. FEWI, pp. 7-8.
117. *American Economic Review*, March 1944. (FEWI, p. 209).
118. Institute on Postwar Reconstruction, *loc. cit.* (FEWI, p. 158.)
119. *Christian Science Monitor*, July 23, 1949. (FEWI, p. 151.)
120. IFE, pp. 24-25.
121. IFE, p. 24.
122. Institute on Postwar Reconstruction, *loc. cit.*
123. IFE, pp. 22-23.
124. Radio broadcast, February 1975. (FEWI, p. 55.)
125. FE, p. 1.
126. *World Economics*, October-December 1945. (FEWI, pp. 182-183.)
127. FEWI, p. 24. (1978) Italics added.
128. Address to Governor of Hawaii's Conference, Honolulu, February 2, 1967. (*Essays*, p. 280.)
129. *Greenwich News*, *loc. cit.*
130. FEWI, p. x.
131. *American Economic Review*, March 1944. (FEWI, p. 211.)
132. FEWI, p. 24. (1978)
133. *Monterey Peninsula Herald*, March 5, 1970. (FEWI, p. 98.)
134. FEWI, p. 23. (1978)
135. *Monterey Peninsula Herald*, March 5, 1970. (FEWI, p. 98.)
136. FEWI, p. 8.
137. FEWI, p. 24. (1978)
138. Governor of Hawaii's Conference, *loc. cit.* (*Essays*, p. 281.)
139. *Congressional Record*, *loc. cit.* (FEWI, p. 70.)
140. *Christian Science Monitor*, *loc. cit.* (FEWI, pp. 150-151.)
141. "This Linkage Needs Attention," unpublished article, 1984.
142. *Ibid.*
143. IFE, p. 205.
144. See *Congressional Record*, *loc. cit.* (FEWI, pp. 70-77.)
145. See *Hearings*, 95th Cong. 1st sess., Washington, D.C.: GPO, 1977, II, 473-79.
146. FEWI, p. x.
147. *Essays*, p. iv.
148. Radio broadcast, February 1975. (FEWI, pp. 54-55.)
149. FEWI, p. 10. First two italics added.
150. FEWI, pp. 10-11.
151. FEWI, pp. 10 and 15.
152. IFE pp. 44-45.
153. FEWI, p. 11.
154. FEWI, p. 50. (1975)
155. *Ibid.*
156. Radio broadcast, February 1975. (FEWI, p. 60.)